LONGMAN BUSINESS ENGLISH S

Meetings and discussions

NINA O'DRISCOLL AND ADRIAN PILBEAM

LONGMAN

SERIES EDITOR NINA O'DRISCOLL
WITH MARK ELLIS AND ADRIAN PILBEAM

The authors work for Language Training Services

Addison Wesley Longman Limited,
Edinburgh Gate, Harlow
Essex CM20 2JE, England
and Associated Companies throughout the world

© Mark Ellis, Nina O'Driscoll and Adrian Pilbeam 1987
Published jointly by Studentlitteratur AB, Lund, Sweden
and Longman Group UK Limited, London, England.

First published 1987
First published in colour 1992
Seventh impression 1998

ISBN 0 582 09305 8

Set in 9/11pt Linotron 202 Helvetica

Printed in China
EPC/07

Acknowledgements

We are grateful to the following for their permission to
reproduce copyright photographs:

Ace Photo Agency for page 40; The Image Bank for pages 33
and 42; Tony Stone Worldwide for pages 6, 24, 36 and 51; The
Telegraph Colour Library for page 14, 16, 29, 59, 60 and 68.

Cover Photograph by The Telegraph Colour Library.

Contents

INTRODUCTION TO THE LEARNER

Meetings and discussions is part of the Longman Business Skills series. It presents and practises the language used by people in business meetings and discussions. The book consists of extracts from company business meetings where three to five people are involved, both native and non-native speakers. All of the subjects discussed are controversial ones that give rise to different opinions, and the full range of argumentation language is presented. Practice in using this language follows each extract.

Objectives

The aim of this book is

- to help you recognize the way arguments and opinions can be built up for use in discussions.
- to improve your listening skills in this area.
- to help you build up your own ability to present and argue points of view in discussions.

Contents

The book consists of eight units. Each unit covers a different aspect of the language of meetings, ranging from starting a meeting, presenting and supporting opinions, to summarizing and concluding. Each unit consists of extracts of meetings on cassette, followed by questions that check comprehension and focus attention on particular language features. Then comes presentation of the main language points in the unit, followed by practice activities of both a closed and open-ended style. All of these practice activities are on the cassette.

Using the book

The units can be used in sequence, to build up the full range of discussion skills, or in isolation if you want to concentrate on only one aspect, eg *making suggestions.* There is no continuous storyline running through the book, although the same basic situation reappears in each block of two units.

THE LISTENING PHASE

This covers the first three parts of each unit – **Comprehension Check, Focus on Language,** and **Focus on Intention.** It involves listening several times to the extract of a meeting, each time for a different purpose. The aim is to develop your recognition of the language used in argumentation.

LANGUAGE SUMMARIES   These follow the listening phase, and are clear presentations of the main kind of language relevant to that unit, eg *to accept ideas and proposals, to support an argument.*

PRACTICES   These follow each language summary. They are designed to activate and practise the language presented in the unit. This is mainly done on cassette, where you have to expand some notes into a short argument to support an opinion or to reject a proposal. . . .etc. You then compare your version with the model version on the tape. All material on cassette is marked ▭ in the book. Some of these practice activities are very controlled, and in that case your version should be similar to the model version. Other activities are very open-ended, and you have to develop your own opinions about a point. In this case your version could be very different from the model version. The model version is only ever a suggestion – there will always be other ways to say the same thing. If your version is different it will not be wrong if it has the same style and form as the model version.

Working alone   If you are using this book by yourself, try to record your versions of the practice activities on cassette. If this is difficult to do, say them aloud and then write them down so that you can compare them with the model versions later. Each question in the book, from the comprehension check to the practice activities, has an answer in the key. All of the model versions of the practice activities are on cassette, as well as written out in the key.

Working with a teacher   If you can practise the activities with a teacher and other friends and colleagues, you will be able to have more realistic short discussions and exchanges of opinion in the practice activities. It will be less necessary to record your versions and to use the key.

1 Starting and controlling meetings

Aims   This unit looks at the language used by the person chairing a meeting or discussion

- to open the discussion and introduce the items to be discussed
- to summarize the main facts of a case

Background   Six months ago *flexitime* was introduced in the administrative and personnel departments of INCA, the UK subsidiary of an American engineering company which produces lifts. Initially, the scheme seemed to be very successful and extremely popular in both departments. But now the employees in the production departments are beginning to object and demand a similar system for themselves. One department has just started a ban on all overtime as a protest. The company is especially keen to avoid any further confrontation as order books are full and there is the chance of a major contract with the Middle East.

 Comprehension Check   Listen to this extract from a meeting held to discuss this problem. Taking part in the meeting, in order of speaking, are:

Managing Director, Graham Burns.
Production Manager, Bob Clark.
Personnel Manager, Anne Byron.

Decide if the following statements are **true** or **false**.

1   The company is about to launch a new product.

2   The Managing Director, who speaks first, wants to introduce flexitime for all departments in the company.

3   The Production Manager, who speaks second, also wants his people to have flexitime.

4   Everyone in the company works forty hours a week.

5   The Personnel Manager agrees to stop the flexitime arrangement in her department.

> Check your answers in the key.

Focus on Language   Listen to the extract again and answer the following questions about the language used.

1   What words does the Managing Director use to open the meeting?

2   Before stating the objectives of the meeting he summarizes the background to the problem which they are all familiar with. What words does he use to introduce this summary?

3   There are two objectives to the meeting:
   ●   to look into ways of avoiding any further industrial action.
   ●   to review the whole situation regarding flexitime.

What phrase does he use to introduce the two objectives?
Complete the sentence:

_____ _____ _____ _____ _____

firstly to . . . and secondly to. . .

4 After opening the meeting he directs the meeting to the
Production Manager, Bob Clark. What exactly does he
say?

_____ , Bob _____ _____

_____ _____

_____ .

5 When the Production Manager suggests that office
workers do exactly as they please, the Personnel
Manager interrupts suddenly. What expression does she
use to do this?

6 The Managing Director then overrules the interruption.
What phrase does he use? Complete the sentence:

_____ _____

_____ , *let Bob finish. . .*

7 Near the end of the meeting the Managing Director feels
that the discussion is getting away from the subject.
   a How does he state this? Complete the sentence:

   Look, _____ _____ _____

   _____ *interesting but* _____

   _____ _____

   b How does he restate the main objective of the
   meeting? Complete the sentence:

   _____ _____ _____

   _____ _____ *flexitime is a valid concept*
   _____ *how we're going to avoid a strike.*

> Check your
> answers in the key.

Focus on   The full text of the extract is given below, divided into three
Intention   sections. At the beginning of each section is a list of the
different speakers' intentions – what each speaker is trying
to do or say at each stage in the discussion, eg *open the
meeting* or *present a summary of the problem.*

Match each intention with the corresponding part of the
discussion. Some intentions have been marked as
examples.

SECTION 1   **SPEAKERS' INTENTIONS**

Opens the meeting.
Directs the meeting to the first speaker.

States the objectives of the meeting.
Presents a summary of the problem.

INTENTION

| Managing Director | *Right. Let's get started.* | a | Opens the meeting. |

As you know, we're just about to launch a major new product. But yesterday I was approached by a representative of our union, demanding an introduction of flexitime for their members and threatening some kind of go-slow. One department has already banned overtime and I'm afraid that we could have a strike on our hands before long.

b _____

I've called this meeting firstly to look into ways of avoiding any further industrial action and secondly to review the whole situation regarding flexitime.

c States the objectives of the meeting.

Perhaps you'd like to start, Bob, and put us in the picture.

d _____

SECTION 2   SPEAKERS' INTENTIONS

Restates the problem.
Counters criticism by explaining the situation.
Criticizes.
Returns to the original explanation of the problem.
Interrupts to check the implications.
Interrupts to control the meeting.

INTENTION

Production Manager	*Well, Graham this morning I spent three hours with the unions and basically they want the same privileges as our administrative people. Frankly I don't blame them. They resent the fact that anybody with an office job can do exactly as they please.*	a	_____
Personnel Manager	*Hold on, what do you mean by that? Are you implying. . .*	b	Interrupts to check the implications.
Managing Director	*Just a minute, Anne, let Bob finish what he was saying. We'll come to your point later.*	c	_____
Production Manager	*Anyway, as I was saying, my people resent the fact that your department can walk in at ten in the morning when we've already done half a day's work.*	d	_____
	We have to be in the factory at seven, but your people can do exactly what they want.	e	_____
Personnel Manager	*What do you mean by that? You know very well that everybody works forty hours. The only difference is that they can come in any time between seven and ten.*	f	_____

SECTION 3   **SPEAKERS' INTENTIONS**

Explains rejection in greater detail.
Rejects a suggestion.
Claims irrelevance. (2)
Restates objectives.
Puts forward a suggestion.
Criticizes.

		INTENTION
Managing Director	*Look, all this is very interesting but you're missing the point.*	a Claims irrelevance.
	The question is not whether flexitime is a valid concept but how we're going to avoid a strike. Now let's move on.	b _____
	Why can't we introduce flexitime in your production department?	c _____
Production Manager	*Well it's not that I've got anything against flexitime but you really can't introduce it at shop floor level.*	d _____
	We have to keep the assembly line moving at all times and it just wouldn't be possible to have people coming in when they please. The plant is old and any changes would mean extensive redesign.	e _____
Personnel Manager	*I'm sorry but that's hardly my problem.*	f _____
	You can't expect me to drop a system just because you can't find ways of adapting. . .	g Criticizes.

> Check your answers in the key.

Language Summary 1

Opening a meeting

A lot of this extract shows the Managing Director opening and directing the meeting. Some useful phrases to use here are given below.

a   Starting a meeting

Well, ladies and gentlemen, I think we should begin.

Perhaps we'd better get started/get down to business.

Right then, I think it's about time we got started/going.

Right then, I think we should begin.

Let's begin/get going, shall we?

Shall we start?

b   Stating objectives

The purpose of this meeting is, first, to. . .and secondly to. . .

We are here today to consider firstly. . .secondly. . . thirdly. . .

The main objective of our meeting is. . .

I've called this meeting first to. . .secondly to. . .

c Keeping the meeting moving

Would you like to begin/to open the discussion. . .?

Perhaps you'd like to explain/tell us/give us. . .

What do you think. . .?

Shall we continue then?

Let's move on.

Would you like to comment here?

What about you?

 PRACTICE 1 Present the following subjects for discussion at a meeting, stating the objectives clearly. After listening to the example on the cassette, make up your own versions for the other subjects.

EXAMPLE

Background	Objectives
Directive from HQ demanding 5% reduction in costs over the next six months.	**a** Identify areas of waste.
	b Come up with some suggestions concerning possible economies.

Right, let's get started. As you may know, we have received a directive from HQ in New York demanding a 5% reduction in costs over the next six months. So I've called this meeting first to identify possible areas of waste, and secondly to get some suggestions about where we should cut back.

Background	Objectives
a Takeover of the company by a big international firm who want to streamline the business.	• Ideas for improving efficiency in the department.
	• Introduction of new technology
b Interviews have to be held for two vacant sales positions.	• Define exactly what we are looking for.
	• Draw up a shortlist of candidates.

c A trade delegation is arriving from Japan next month.

- Agenda for the week.
- Programme of social events.
- Where exactly the delays happen.
- The causes.
- Solutions.

> Compare your versions with the ones in the key. They are on the cassette.

d Several complaints have been received about delivery delays.

Language Summary 2

Summarizing and presenting the main facts of a case

Right at the beginning of the meeting the Managing Director, Graham Burns, summarized the background to the case. Some phrases to use here are:

As some of you probably know,

As you know,

Some months/years ago/yesterday

The situation now is

 PRACTICE 2

Reorganize the information presented below and present it as if you were opening a meeting. Pick out only the facts that you think would be relevant to the objectives of the meeting.

Objective
As Personnel Manager you have called a meeting of management to discuss whether or not one of your junior executives, John Saunders, should be appointed to a more senior post in the company headquarters. The post has been advertised in the national press.

Key facts
Company policy in this multinational company is to send potential management candidates overseas for a minimum of two years to widen their experience.

a Saunders applied for a senior post in headquarters which became vacant last month.

b He is very competent, with excellent results after four years in the company.

c 18 months ago you offered him an overseas posting to North Africa.

d Six months ago you offered him a post in France.

2 Presenting and supporting opinions

Aims   This unit looks at the language and tactics which can be used

- to ask for opinions
- to present and support opinions
- to agree and disagree

e He refused the posting in North Africa due to personal reasons – the ill health of his wife. He asked for a postponement of any overseas placement.

f The Personnel Manager agreed to postpone the posting abroad.

g Three candidates and Saunders have been interviewed but he clearly has the greatest ability.

h Refused the posting to France, his excuse again was the ill health of his wife.

> Compare your version with the one in the key. It is on the cassette.

 PRACTICE 3   Reorganize the information and present it as if you were opening a meeting. Pick out only the facts that you think would be relevant to the objective of the meeting.

Objective
As the owner of a small company, you have called a meeting to discuss what to do about one of your staff, Anne Smith, who has recently expressed dissatisfaction with the job and is thinking of leaving. You are looking for suggestions to make her change her mind.

Key Facts
The company is new and small and cannot afford to give high salaries.

a She joined the company two years ago.

b She has worked very hard and usually produced good results.

c You are unwilling to replace her as the company is small and very busy and you don't want to spend additional time training a replacement.

d She knows a lot about many aspects of the company and it would take time for any new staff to obtain such a wide knowledge of the company.

e Recently you have noticed she has been unable to meet deadlines and is generally less enthusiastic and hardworking than before.

f Two weeks ago she came to you and presented the following complaints:
pressures too great.
job taking up too much personal time.
no time for friends or family.
working until 8 pm and some weekends.
salary not high enough.

> Compare your version with the one in the key. It is on the cassette.

Background   After several years of low profits and intensive competition from larger chemical companies, Agrolux, a medium-sized company which produces agricultural products such as fertilizers and pesticides is facing a choice between a definitely profitable contract with the government to carry out research and develop chemical products for the Ministry of Defence, or alternatively following up some initial but successful research into ways of speeding up plant growth. The second choice, if successful, would be a major scientific breakthrough and could in the long run be very profitable for the company. The decision has been further complicated by an information leak to the press about the company's possible future involvement in the Defence sector.

 Comprehension Check   The meeting you will hear on cassette took place after a difficult public meeting at which the company tried to explain its position. Taking part in the meeting, in order of speaking, are:

Managing Director, Nigel Scott.
Marketing Manager, John Davis.
Head of Research, Philip Lucas.
Financial Director, Helen Carlton.

Decide if the following statements are **true** or **false**.

1   The Marketing Manager supports the profitable government product.

2   There is another company which produces both types of product.

3   The Managing Director believes the company should not try to do too many projects at once.

4   The Head of Research wants to avoid the government project at all costs.

5   The Financial Director feels that the company's shareholders would support the more profitable choice of the government contract.

> Check your
> answers in the key.

Focus on Language   Listen to the extract again and answer the following questions about the language used.

1   How does the Managing Director ask for the Marketing Manager's opinion at the beginning of the meeting? What words does he use?

_____   _____   _____   _____

on this government contract, John?

2   What word tells you that the Marketing Manager is speaking only for himself when he gives his opinion?

3 How does the Head of Research indicate his disagreement with the Marketing Manager? Is it a strong or weak disagreement?

4 The Managing Director then gives his opinion about getting involved in several things at once. How does he introduce this? Is it a strong or weak opinion?

_____ _____ _____ _____ _____

rush into things.

5 The Managing Director then supports his point of view with two reasons. How does he distinguish between them?

It'll mean _____ _____ a huge injection of cash _____ _____ a large extension of our existing research facilities.

6 The Managing Director then disagrees with the accusation by the Head of Research that he is afraid to take risks. What are his opening words that show he disagrees?

7 The Head of Research puts forward his opinion about what the company should do. How does he introduce his opinion? Is it very strong?

_____ _____ _____ _____

_____ *that's the direction we have to go in.*

8 Does the Financial Director agree or disagree with this statement? What does she say?

Check your answers in the key.

Focus on Intention

The full text of the extract is given below, divided into three sections. At the beginning of each section there is a list of the different speakers' intentions – what each speaker is trying to do or say at each stage in the discussion.

Match each intention with the corresponding part of the discussion. Some intentions have been marked as examples.

SECTION 1   **SPEAKERS' INTENTIONS**

Disagrees.
Asks for an opinion.
Expands his point of view. (2)
Gives an opinion. (2)

		INTENTION
Managing Director	*What are your feelings on this government contract, John?*	a Asks for an opinion.
Marketing Manager	*Well, personally I think we've got to avoid any contract which involves us with the Ministry of Defence.*	b _____
	I mean we've got to consider public opinion.	c _____
Head of Research	*I disagree completely. You're being too emotional about the whole thing. We've got to look at this objectively.*	d Disagrees.
	As I see it, we're faced with a straight business decision.	e _____
	It's a choice between immediate but short term profits with the government, and, on the other hand, developing a risky new product that may never earn the company any money.	f _____

SECTION 2   **SPEAKERS' INTENTIONS**

Restates his views.
Explains his point of view.
Explains negative consequences.
Disagrees. (2)
Gives some evidence to support his case.
Criticizes.
Expresses reservation about an idea.

		INTENTION
Financial Director	*And why not both?*	a Disagrees.
	Take the case of Neco. They're involved in both types of business.	b _____

Managing Director	*Yes, but you've got to remember that Neco is four times our size.*	c	_____
	I'm convinced we shouldn't rush into things that we may not be capable of doing. In my view, trying to develop in too many directions would be madness.	d	_____
	It'll mean not only a huge injection of cash but also a large extension of our existing research facilities and we just don't have the money at the moment.	e	_____
Head of Research	*In other words, you won't take the risk.*	f	_____
Managing Director	*On the contrary Philip, I'm only trying to do what is best for the company.*	g	_____
	We may be relatively small, but we do have a reputation for quality and I'm sure we'll lose it if we get involved in too many projects.	h	Restates his views.

SECTION 3   SPEAKERS' INTENTIONS

Argues an opinion.
Expresses reservation.
Agrees.
Supports a point of view.
Closes the meeting.

INTENTION

Head of Research	*Maybe,*	a	Expresses reservation.
	but if there's more profit in going ahead with the government project, it seems to me that that's the direction we have to go in.	b	_____
Financial Director	*Exactly.*	c	_____
	You've got to think of our shareholders too. They're not going to accept years of low profits when they know you've had the chance of a contract that guarantees immediate profits for the next two years.	d	_____
Managing Director	*Well, I think we all need to think more about this whole matter, so I suggest we stop here and meet again tomorrow at eleven.*	e	_____

> Check your answers in the key.

Language Summary 1

Opinions

a Asking for opinions

At the beginning of the meeting the Managing Director asks the Marketing Manager for his opinion on the government contract. He uses the phrase.

What are your feelings on this?

Expressions to get someone's opinions can be directed specifically at one person eg *What do you think about. . .?* or they can be directed at a group of people in general eg *What's the general feeling on. . .?*

Other phrases that can be used here are:

To one person	To a group of people
What are your views on. . .?	*Any reaction to that?*
What are your feelings about. . .?	*Has anybody any strong feeling about/views on that?*
What do you think about. . .?	*What's the general view on/feeling about that?*
What's your opinion about that?	*Has anybody any comments to make?*

b Giving opinions

During the meeting a number of people gave opinions about the subject being discussed.

An opinion can be expressed in a *strong* way, in a *neutral* way (the most common) or *tentatively* (with some hesitation or reservation). Tentative opinions are very typical of British people. Americans would usually be more positive.

Phrases that can be used are:

Strong	Neutral	Tentative
I'm sure that. . .	*I think/I believe that. . .*	*It seems to me that. . .*
I'm convinced that. . .	*As I see it. . .*	*I'm inclined to think that. . .*
I feel quite sure that. . .	*From a financial point of view. . .*	*My inclination would be to. . .*
It's perfectly clear to me that. . .	*The way I see it is that. . .*	*I tend to favour the view that. . .*

PRACTICE 1 Listen to the extract from the meeting again and pick out the phrases that signal each speaker's opinion and match these with the statements in the right hand column. Decide whether the opinion is **strong**, **neutral** or **tentative**. The first one has been done as an example.

		Signal	**Information**
a	Marketing Manager	*Personally I think* **(neutral)**	*we've got to avoid any contract which involves us with the Ministry of Defence.*
b	Head of Research	_____	*we're faced with a straight business decision.*
c	Managing Director	_____	*we shouldn't rush into things. . .*
d	Managing Director	_____	*trying to develop in too many directions would be madness.*
e	Managing Director	_____	*we'll lose it* (our reputation) *if we get involved in too many projects.*
f	Head of Research	_____	*that's the direction we have to go in.*

> Check your answers in the key.

PRACTICE 2 Give opinions on the following points according to the prompts in brackets. Try and support your opinion with some kind of justification or some evidence. Listen to the first example on the tape.

EXAMPLE
Drinking and driving **(strong)**
– must be avoided.

It's perfectly clear to me that drinking and driving is dangerous and must be avoided.

a Expense account lunches **(neutral)**
– cost to the company.

b "Gifts" as a method for securing orders **(neutral)**
– bad business practice – accepted custom in some countries.

c Companies which have adopted a policy of stopping all new recruitment as the main way to reduce costs and survive a crisis **(tentative)**
– shortsighted view of the problem.

d The introduction of a system in which everyone in a company, from top to bottom, clocks in **(tentative)**
  – system is democratic.

e The belief that more and more manufacturing industries will be transferred to the Far East because of lower labour costs **(strong)**
  – lower labour costs.

f The view that by the year 2000 world oil reserves will be running out and most of the energy will be supplied by nuclear power **(neutral)**
  – most energy supplied by nuclear power.

> Compare your versions with the ones in the key. They are on the cassette.

Language Summary 2

Disagreeing and agreeing

When the Marketing Manager says he is against the government contract, the Head of Research disagrees, using the phrase *I disagree completely.*

When we agree with someone the expression we choose will indicate to the listener the strength of our opinion. Sometimes we neither agree nor disagree but want to express only certain reservations.

Phrases that can be used to agree or disagree are:

Agreement	
STRONG	**NEUTRAL**
I'm in complete agreement.	*I agree.*
I quite agree.	*You're right there.*
I couldn't agree more.	*I think you're right.*
Yes, definitely.	*Yes, and. . .*
Exactly!	*That's true.*
Precisely.	*That's right.*

Disagreement	
STRONG	**NEUTRAL**
I disagree completely.	*I don't agree.*
That's out of the question.	*That's not how I see it.*
On the contrary.	*I wouldn't say that.*
Of course not!	*I think you're wrong.*
That's ridiculous.	*I disagree.*

Expressing reservations and doubts
I agree up to a point but. . .
I see your point but. . .
That's true but. . .
I suppose you're right but. . .
Yes, but. . .
Maybe but. . .

PRACTICE 3 Listen to the meeting again and decide if the responses to the following statements are agreements (A), disagreements (D) or expressions of reservation (R), and whether they are strong (S) or neutral (N). Note down the phrase used for the response. The first one has been done as an example.

	Statement		Response
Marketing Manager	*I think we've got to avoid any contract which involves us with the Ministry of Defence.*	a	*I disagree completely. (D/S)*
Financial Director	*Why not both?* (projects)	b	_____
Head of Research	*You won't take the risk.* (The MD is unwilling to follow up both plans.)	c	_____
Managing Director	*We'll lose it* (our reputation) *if we get involved in too many projects.*	d	_____
Head of Research	*If there's more profit in going ahead with the government project, it seems to me that that's the direction we have to go in.*	e	_____

Check your answers in the key.

PRACTICE 4 Respond to the following comments as instructed. Make sure you justify your point of view. Listen to the example first.

EXAMPLE

A *If there aren't enough jobs around, the number of university places should be reduced. There's no point educating people for the unemployment queue.*
Disagree: more people for higher education – importance of subjects like engineering and computing.

B *I'm afraid I disagree. We need more people to receive higher education, but they need to study the right subjects like engineering and computing.*

a *If you want to reduce inflation the only solution is a strict control of the money supply.*
Express reservation: strong wage and price controls also possible.

b *There's no point in training as a secretary these days. With all the new technology for the office the job won't exist in ten years.*
Disagree: type of work will change – more like a personal assistant.

c *The best jobs for the future will be in the service and food industries.*
Agree: bad future for manufacturing industries.

d *If everyone agreed to take a reduction in wages we'd solve the unemployment problem in Europe within a year.*
Disagree: problem more complex.

e *Unless you're a teacher or a secretary, there just aren't enough chances for women to get responsible jobs.*
Express reservation: things slowly changing.

f *Introducing a 35 hour week might be a good idea from the employee's point of view but it would be a disaster from the company's point of view.*
Agree: costs up – no increase in productivity.

> Compare your versions with the ones in the key. They are on the cassette.

3 Balancing points of view

Aims   This unit looks at the language used
- to present a balanced point of view
- to point out consequences

Background

In Unit 2, senior members of Agrolux, a medium sized chemical company, discussed the choice they had to make between a profitable government contract to research and develop products for the Ministry of Defence and their own research project to develop ways of speeding up plant growth. The government project offered certain profits but had clear ethical and image problems. The second solution was preferable but not financially certain. The general opinion at the first meeting was divided. Now, a day later, they have had the opportunity to think more about the dilemma, and this is reflected in the style of discussion and some of the opinions.

 Comprehension Check

Listen to the extract from this second meeting. The same people are involved, and they speak in the following order:

Head of Research, Philip Lucas.
Managing Director, Nigel Scott.
Marketing Manager, John Davis.
Financial Director, Helen Carlton.

Answer the following questions about the opinions expressed by the different members of the meeting.

1 Is the Head of Research still 100% in favour of the government project?

2 Why is the Managing Director against the government project?

3 Which project does the Marketing Manager think will be more profitable?

4 What are the disadvantages of the government project?

5 Which of the projects is described as a *gamble*?

> Check your answers in the key.

Focus on Language

Listen to the extract again and answer the following questions about the language used.

1 How does the Head of Research show that he understands the arguments of the person who spoke before him? What are his words?

_____ _____ _____ _____

_____ _____ *the problems with our image,*
but. . .

2 The Managing Director tries to balance the arguments of the two sides. How does he point out a disadvantage of the Head of Research's opinion?

Yes, _____ _____ _____
_____ _____ *it would*
demand a lot of extra work. . .

3 He then adds another reason against the government project. How does he introduce this additional reason?

And _____ _____ , we wouldn't have either the resources. . .

4 The Marketing Manager then adds another reason in favour of the plant growth research project. What word introduces this other reason?

5 How does he point out a consequence of taking the government project?

. . . but_____ _____ _____

_____ _____ _____

and the project is cancelled or frozen, _____

_____ _____ with nothing at all.

6 The Financial Director tries to take a more practical, business-like approach. He balances the possible success of the plant growth project with the financial risks involved. What does he say?

_____ this work on plant growth rates _____ succeed eventually, it's too much of a gamble. . .

> Check your answers in the key.

Focus on Intention   The full text of the extract is given below, divided into three sections as before. At the beginning of each section there is a list of the different speakers' intentions – what each one is trying to say at each stage in the discussion in order to develop his argument.

Match each intention with the corresponding part of the discussion. Some intentions have been marked as examples.

SECTION 1   **SPEAKERS' INTENTIONS**

Gives an additional reason.
Gives his reason.
Shows understanding of another point of view.
Points out a disadvantage.
Puts forward an opposite point of view.

		INTENTION
Head of Research	*I accept what you say about the problems with our image,*	a _____
	but I still feel that this government project could be very interesting for us.	b _____

Managing Director	*Yes, but on the other hand it would demand a lot of extra work on our part.*	c _____
	There would be continual reports, meetings, checks and cross-checks which would waste hours of everybody's time and create all kinds of extra administration.	d Gives his reason.
	And what's more, we wouldn't have either the resources or money to pursue our own projects.	e _____

SECTION 2   SPEAKERS' INTENTIONS

Adds an extra reason.
Points out a possible consequence.
Shows agreement.
Adds an extra disadvantage.

INTENTION

Marketing Manager	*Yes, I agree totally with Nigel.*	a _____
	Moreover, you've got to see that there's much more long term profit in developing the plant growth project.	b _____
	Of course, taking up the government offer may give a more immediate solution to our financial problem, but if there's a change in government policy and the project is cancelled or frozen we'll be left with nothing at all.	c _____
	And another thing, we'll be getting into an area which is very dubious from an ethical point of view.	d Adds an extra disadvantage.

SECTION 3   SPEAKERS' INTENTIONS

Balances an advantage against a disadvantage.
Presents a firm opinion.
Disagrees.
Shows negative consequences.
Summarizes.

INTENTION

Financial Director	*I'm afraid you're being impractical, John.*	a _____
	Although this work on plant growth rates may succeed eventually, it's too much of a gamble for us.	b _____
	If we concentrate all our energies in that direction we'll have to be prepared for unimpressive profits for at least the next few years, and even then there's no guarantee of success.	c Shows negative consequences.
	Quite frankly, I don't think we'll survive that long without money coming in from other sources.	d _____

<table>
<tr><td>Managing
Director</td><td>*Can I come in here Helen? We seem to be losing sight of our objectives. If the company was in a real financial mess I'd have to agree with you – however, as I see it, it's more a question of poor profits rather than a life and death struggle and the question is do we go for short term gains or look for a longer term strategy?*</td></tr>
</table>

e Summarizes.

Check your
answers in the key.

**Language
Summary 1**

Balancing advantages and disadvantages

The members of the meeting are much more reasonable and more prepared to listen to other opinions than in the first meeting (See Unit 2). They try to look at both sides of the problem, balancing advantages and disadvantages.

I accept what you say. . . **but I still feel the government project could be very interesting.**

Although *it may succeed eventually,* **it's too much of a gamble.**

Other phrases that can be used to present a balanced point of view are:

The project would be very profitable. **On the other hand, it would be bad for our image.**

The research project is very interesting from a scientific point of view. **However we wouldn't be able to fund it.**

Note: In all the above examples the part of the sentence which is in **bold italic** represents the final opinion of the speaker.

PRACTICE 1

Combine the following advantages (+) and disadvantages (−) to produce a balanced opinion. Follow the example.

EXAMPLE

(+)	(−)
Government project could be very interesting	Will involve a lot of extra security procedures

Of course, the government project could be very interesting. **On the other hand,** *it will involve a lot of extra security procedures.*

(+)	(−)
a Relocation of offices to smaller centres creates a better working environment.	Recruitment can be more difficult.
b The fall in interest rates makes borrowing cheaper and is good for industry.	Affects the exchange rates which makes essential imports like oil more expensive.

Compare your versions with the ones in the key. They are on the cassette.

c Rationalizing traditional heavy industries like steel or coal improves productivity.

It creates an unemployment problem.

d Import controls help national industries and domestic manufacturers.

They can encourage domestic manufacturers to become uncompetitive.

 PRACTICE 2 Respond to the following opinions by disagreeing, and then present an advantage (+) and disadvantage (−) of that opinion. Give more weight to the disadvantage. Follow the example.

EXAMPLE

Opinion	(+)	(−)
Interest rates should be lowered	more investment	increases spending power and pushes inflation up

Personally I'm not in favour of lower interest rates. I can accept that they create more investment but I feel, more importantly, that they also push up inflation by increasing spending power.

Opinion	(+)	(−)
a More robots should be introduced in industry	increase productivity	lead to unacceptable levels of unemployment
b Direct taxation should be increased	create more revenue for the government	decrease the motivation of companies and individuals
c Exchange controls should be relaxed	encourage international trade and investment	allow money to leave the country for investment abroad
d Flexitime should be more common in companies	give employees more independence	create administrative and staffing problems

Compare your versions with the ones in the key. They are on the cassette.

Language Summary 2

Pointing out consequences

Most of the speakers in the meeting at Agrolux supported their opinions by showing the consequences of different choices.

*If we concentrate all our energies in that direction, **we'll have to be prepared** for unimpressive profits. . .*

The consequences that are pointed out may be certain, as in the example above, or possible.

The following phrases can be used.

Certain Consequences
*Taking the government project **will create/cause** extra security problems.*

*The Ministry of Defence project **will lead to** problems in the public relations field.*

Possible Consequences
*If we do our own research project, it **may create** financial problems.*

*The government project **could cause** all kinds of problems with our public image.*

Note: To indicate what is possible rather than certain use *may* or *could* instead of *will*.

PRACTICE 3

Complete the following dialogue according to the notes in the margin.

Managing Director

So the general conclusion seems to be that (a) _____ we get involved with this government project (b) _____ more problems than it solves.

certain consequence

Marketing Manager

Yes, and it (c) _____ even be bad financially because we'll need to introduce a lot of expensive security measures.

possible consequence

Financial Director

Well, I'm afraid I still disagree. I think the other research project (d) _____ problems of cash flow.

certain consequence

And (e) _____ they get really bad we (f) _____ be forced to cancel the whole project at some future date.

possible consequence

> Check your answers in the key.

PRACTICE 4   Read the following summary of a company problem, and use the information and your own experience to comment on the effects of the proposals that follow.

This company manufactures wallpaper and paints. Four months ago their Research and Development department carried out routine stability tests on one of their quick drying wallpaper pastes. Results indicated that one of the fast dry-up compounds could be harmful. Tests at high temperatures had detected the presence of a vapour known to cause skin conditions. The implication is that wallpaper applied with this paste could be dangerous to health in centrally heated conditions. However further tests have been carried out recently and the results are still inconclusive. Small quantities of this paste are already on the market. Unfortunately there is a rumour in the company that a dangerous substance is being produced. What should the management do?

Proposal EXAMPLE

Ignore the findings completely.
If they ignore the findings from the tests, the rumours may grow and eventually the story will reach the press.

Proposals

a   Stop production immediately and recall all supplies.

b   Ask for more investigation into the chemical but maintain production.

c   Hold a meeting with all employees to tell them of the situation.

d   Write an article in the house journal denying everything.

> Compare your versions with the ones in the key. They are on the cassette.

Language Summary 3

Supporting opinions with a series of consequences

In many cases during the meeting the speakers gave more than one consequence to support their opinions.

*There would be continual reports, checks. . . **and what's more,** we wouldn't have either the resources or money to pursue our own projects.*

*. . . if there is a change in government policy. . . we'll be left with nothing at all. **And another thing,** we'll be getting into an area which is very dubious. . .*

Other phrases to use to present a series of consequences are:

*We can't concentrate all our attention on the government contract. **Not only** will it create a lot of extra work **but it will also** give us a bad image.*

*It's going to involve a lot of extra work on our part **and in addition** it will give us a bad image.*

*It's going to involve a lot of extra work and **apart from that/besides that** it will give us a bad image.*

 PRACTICE 5

Develop the opinions below, giving a series of reasons or consequences for your point of view. Follow the example.

EXAMPLE

Opinions	Reasons
It's much better to send important information by telex, electronic mail or telefax than letter.	Quicker Safer

It's much better to send important information by telex, electronic mail or telefax, than by letter. First of all, it's far quicker, and what's more, it's safer.

a	*Word processors are more efficient than typewriters.*	Can change text easily You can store information
b	*There should be less emphasis on nuclear power.*	Danger of accidents Problem of waste material
c	*Companies should think more about reducing their energy consumption.*	High price of oil and electricity Long term danger of using up oil stocks
d	*I'm against open plan offices.*	Noisy A lot of distractions

> Compare your versions with the ones in the key. They are on the cassette.

4 Making suggestions

Aims   This unit looks at language used

- to make suggestions and recommendations
- to ask for suggestions

Background
Societé de Boissons Gazeuses, a well established French company with about a 15% share of the French soft drinks market, has just been bought by Anker (France), the subsidiary of a large Canadian soft drinks company. Together the combined group will have 25% of the French market. The problem is that the two companies have many similar job functions and production plants located in different parts of France. It is going to be necessary for some rationalization to take place, and some people may be forced to leave the new company, to be called Boissons Anker.

 Comprehension Check
Listen to the extract from a meeting held to discuss the problem. Taking part in the meeting, in order of speaking, are:

European Commercial Manager, Andrew Simmonds.
Marketing Manager (Anker France), Hervé Dalbert.
Marketing Manager (Societé de Boissons Gazeuses), René Labory.

Decide if the following statements are **true** or **false.**

1 The discussion is about which marketing strategy to adopt.

2 The Anker Marketing Manager, who speaks second, wants a two division marketing structure.

3 The existing structure of Societé de Boissons Gazeuses is based on two divisions.

4 The argument against three divisions is that they are more expensive than two.

5 The argument in favour of three divisions is that the service to customers is more personal.

6 There is no difference in terms of the cost of sales between the two systems.

> Check your
> answers in the key.

Focus on Language
Listen to the extract again, and answer the following questions about the language used.

1 The European Commercial Manager does not impose his ideas on the meeting. He wants to get ideas and suggestions from the other people. What does he say? Complete the sentence.

_____ _____ _____ _____

_____ _____ *your suggestions.*

2 How does he bring the first person into the discussion? Complete the sentence.

_____ _____ _____ _____

_____ _____, *Hervé?*

3 Hervé makes a suggestion about the new group
marketing structure. What does he say?

_____ _____ _____ _____

the new group marketing structure _____ *reflect
the existing Anker one.*

4 How does the European Commercial Manager bring
René into the discussion. What does he say?

_____ _____ _____ _____

_____ *René?*

5 René disagrees with Hervé's suggestion.

  a Does he do this politely or aggressively?

  b What are his words?

_____ _____ _____ _____

_____ _____ *Hervé.*

6 René makes another suggestion, and he does this
in a firm, strong way. What are his words?

So _____ _____ _____

_____ *the new company* _____

_____ _____ *on our two division structure.*

7 The European Commercial Manager tries to get Hervé's
reaction to one of René's points.

  a Which of the two opinions does the European
Commercial Manager appear to favour?

  b How does he phrase his question to Hervé? Complete
the sentence.

_____ _____ _____ _____

*your three division structure might be more
expensive. . .?*

8 René, still very diplomatic, suggests a comparison of the
cost of sales for the two companies. How does he
introduce his suggestion?

. . .it _____ _____ _____

_____ _____ *to compare the cost of sales.*

9 René suggests strongly that his company's system
is better. How does he do this? Complete the sentence.

I'm _____ _____ *would prove that the
two division structure* _____ _____

_____ _____

> Check your
> answers in the key.

Focus on Intention

The full text of the extract is given below, divided into three sections. At the beginning of each section there is a list of the different speakers' intentions – what each one is trying to do or say at each stage in the discussion.

Match each intention with the corresponding part of the discussion.

SECTION 1

SPEAKERS' INTENTIONS

Introduces the topic for discussion.
Makes a recommendation.
Requests suggestions.
Invites someone to speak.
Gives preliminary objectives for the meeting.
Gives background information.

INTENTION

European Commercial Manager	*As you know, we have to take some hard decisions about the size and shape of the new company,*	a Gives preliminary objectives for the meeting.
	and I'd like to hear some of your suggestions.	b _____
	First of all, about the reorganization of the marketing department.	c _____
	Can you give us the background, Hervé?	d _____
Marketing Manager (Anker)	*Yes, well you all know that Anker (France) is divided into three divisions for marketing purposes – retail, that's shops and supermarkets; bars and cafés; and restaurants and large hotels. Societé de Boissons Gazeuses on the other hand, has only two divisions – retail; and bars, cafés, restaurants and hotels.*	e Gives background information.
	Our suggestion is that the new group marketing structure should reflect the existing Anker one.	f _____

SECTION 2   **SPEAKERS' INTENTIONS**

Disagrees.
Makes a recommendation.
Supports his argument.
Requests an opinion.
Summarizes his opinion.
Explains his reason for disagreement.

INTENTION

European
Commercial
Manager

What's your reaction to that, René?   a _____

Marketing
Manager
(Strasbourg)

I'm afraid I don't agree with Hervé.   b _____

*The main point of this meeting is to look at ways of
rationalizing the company, and in my opinion the two
division structure that we have is much more efficient than
Anker's three.*   c Explains his
reason for
disagreement.

*But there's no real difference between the bar and café
sector, and restaurants and hotels – the form of distribution
is the same, so is the packaging.*   d _____

*We think that the three division structure has too many
overlaps.*   e Summarizes his
opinion.

*So we strongly recommend that the new company should
be modelled on our two division structure.*   f _____

SECTION 3   **SPEAKERS' INTENTIONS**

Asks for confirmation of an opinion.
Gives a strong opinion.
Expresses tentative agreement.
Disagrees.
Makes a suggestion.
Gives reasons to support his opinion.

INTENTION

European
Commercial
Manager

*That sounds like a very valid point about overlap of
functions.*   a _____

*Don't you think that your three division structure might be
more expensive to operate, Hervé, especially in a bigger
company?*   b Asks for
confirmation of an
opinion.

Marketing
Manager
(Anker)

I don't think so, Andrew.   c _____

It's just a question of splitting resources into three parts, and it enables us to give each market sector more personal service.

d _____

Marketing Manager (Strasbourg)
Before we take any decision it would be a good idea to compare the cost of sales between the two companies for the different sectors.

e Makes a suggestion.

I'm sure that would prove that the two division structure is the only solution. . .

f _____

> Check your answers in the key.

Language Summary 1

Requesting suggestions and ideas

During the meeting the European Commercial Manager needs to get the opinions and suggestions of the two Marketing Managers about the structure of the new marketing department. He does this in several ways.

a An open request
I'd like to hear some of your suggestions.

b A question directed at one person
What's your reaction to that, René?

c A request for confirmation of his own opinion
Don't you think that your three division structure might be more expensive to operate, Hervé?

Other phrases that can be used here are:

I'd like to hear your ideas on this.

Do any of you have any suggestions?

How do you think we should do this?

What would you suggest?

What do you recommend?

Do you think we should. . .?

Any suggestions?

I suggest we should. . . What do you think?

What are your views on this?

What's your opinion?

How do you see this?

PRACTICE 1   Introduce the following topics for discussion and ask for suggestions. Follow the example.

EXAMPLE

Need to choose a new Computer Manager.
Promote internally or recruit from outside.

Well, as you know, we need to choose a new Computer Manager, and the problem is whether to promote internally or to recruit from outside. I'd like to hear your ideas on this.

a Objective is to improve productivity without extra investment in equipment.

b Problem is to keep pay rises within government limits and to maintain motivation of the workforce at the same time.

c How to expand the business without losing control or borrowing large amounts of money. My idea is franchising.

d There is a proposal to introduce early retirement for all managers over 50 because they are not in tune with new technology. This would leave the company without valuable experience.

e Fuel prices have risen. This affects distribution costs. Should we increase prices?

f The company needs to change its image from that of a traditional safe insurance giant to a dynamic financial services group.

> Compare your versions with the ones in the key. They are on the cassette.

Language Summary 2

Making suggestions and recommendations

The two Marketing Managers both gave suggestions and recommendations about the organization of the marketing activities of the new group. The phrases they used were:

Our suggestion is that the new group marketing structure should reflect the existing Anker one.

We strongly recommend that the new company should be modelled on our two division structure.

Suggestions and recommendations can be **strong, neutral** or **tentative.** Examples of other phrases to use are:

Strong suggestions

The only solution is to. . .

I see no other alternative but to. . .

There is no alternative but to. . .

We must. . .

Neutral suggestions

I recommend that we should. . .

I think we should. . .

My recommendation is that we should. . .

I would suggest that we. . .

We should/ought to. . .

If I were you I would. . .

Tentative suggestions

We could always. . .

It might be a good idea to. . .

Have you thought of _____ ing. . .

One solution would be to. . .

What about _____ ing. . .

PRACTICE 2 Give suggestions and recommendations to respond to the following problems. Follow the example.

EXAMPLE

Problem: Sales of a new electric car have not been as good as predicted, and stocks are high.

Suggestions: 1 Stop production. **(strong)**
2 Cut prices. **(neutral)**

As I see it, we have no alternative but to stop production. In addition, I think we should cut prices to move the stock and improve cashflow.

a Problem: Deliveries of goods have been delayed frequently in recent months, due to rail strikes.

Suggestions: 1 Investigate road transport. **(neutral)**
2 Set up small regional warehouses. **(tentative)**

b Problem: Some tinned fruit sold by a German supermarket and imported from Spain has caused customer complaints.

Suggestions:
1 Withdraw all tins from the shelves. **(strong)**
2 Arrange a meeting with the production people from the Spanish plant. **(neutral)**
3 Send some of our production people to Spain to check quality control. **(tentative)**

c Problem: Your company is trying to take over another company in a similar field. Your bid has been rejected because it is too low. You really want to succeed.

Suggestions:
1 Increase the bid. **(strong)**
2 Try to buy more shares privately. **(neutral)**
3 Write to the other company's shareholders. **(tentative)**

d Problem: A bank has lent $500,000 to a medium sized company for research and development into a new product. However, progress has been slow and the company needs more money to finish the research.

Suggestions:
1 Send a consultant to investigate progress. **(strong)**
2 Establish a deadline for results. **(tentative)**
3 Take a participation in the company. **(tentative)**

e Problem: A newspaper group is having problems with its circulation. Costs are also high for setting and printing.

Suggestions:
1 Hire a new editor. **(neutral)**
2 Negotiate with the print unions to modernize production methods. **(strong)**

> Compare your versions with the ones in the key. They are on the cassette.

5 Presenting alternatives

Aims   This unit looks at language used

- to present a number of different solutions
- to justify choices and solutions
- to contrast alternatives

Background

As we know from Unit 4, Societé de Boissons Gazeuses and Anker (France) have recently merged into one big group to be called Boissons Anker. In addition to the changes in the marketing organization of the company, other changes will have to take place. One of these is the choice of a location for the headquarters of the new group.

Comprehension Check

Listen to the extract from the meeting held to discuss the problem. Taking part in the meeting, in order of speaking, are:

General Manager of the new group, John Petersen.
Personnel Manager (Strasbourg), Martine Reyser.
Personnel Manager (Anker France), Jacques Lutsen.
Financial Manager of the new group, Ken Copeland.

Decide if the following statements are **true** or **false.**

1 The report recommends that the new headquarters should be in Paris.

2 The General Manager is in favour of having a small holding company based in Paris.

3 The Personnel Manager of Societé de Boissons Gazeuses who speaks second, wants to move to Paris.

4 The Personnel Manager of Anker France, who speaks third, suggests that part of the headquarters should be based in Strasbourg.

5 It would be cheaper to have the headquarters in Paris.

6 The Financial Manager, who speaks fourth, does not want to move everything to Paris.

> Check your
> answers in the key.

Focus on Language

Listen to the extract again, and answer the following questions about the language used.

1 The General Manager mentions two possibilities for the location of the headquarters. How does he introduce the first possibility? Complete the sentence.

_____ _____ _____ *to move all headquarters' functions to Paris.*

2 How does he introduce the second possibility? Complete the sentence.

_____ _____ _____ *continue to run the two companies quite separately.*

3 Martine, the Personnel Manager in Strasbourg, is against a move to Paris. She justifies her opinion with two arguments. How does she introduce these arguments? Complete the sentences.

_____ _____ _____ , *we've just completed work on a new headquarters building . . .*

_____ _____ _____

in the eyes of the employees _____ _____
_____ *of people's lives.*

4 Jacques, the Personnel Manager of Anker France tries to open the discussion out, so that other possibilities can be looked at. How does he do this? Complete the sentence.

. . .perhaps we could look at some other options. There

_____ _____ _____ _____

_____ _____ _____ _____

_____ *with the problem.*

5 How does he introduce his first solution?

_____ _____ _____ _____

to move everything to Paris. . .

6 How does he introduce his second solution?

_____ _____ _____ _____

_____ *to separate some of the HQ functions. . .*

7 Martine contrasts the advantage of basing some HQ functions in Strasbourg with the disadvantage of moving everyone to Paris. How does she do this? Complete the sentence.

Keeping some functions in Strasbourg _____
_____ *our recent investment in a new building*

_____ _____ _____

a total move to Paris _____ _____

_____ _____ _____

8 The Financial Manager of the group agrees with Martine. He too weighs the two alternatives of moving to Paris or keeping part of the HQ in Strasbourg. How does he introduce these alternatives and the resulting consequences? Complete the sentence.

_____ *we keep the Paris part of the HQ fairly small and* _____ _____ _____

_____ _____ *we move everything to Paris and* _____ _____ _____

_____ _____ _____

dissatisfaction.

Check your answers in the key.

Focus on Intention   The full text of the extract is given below, divided into four sections. At the beginning of each section there is a list of the different speakers' intentions – what each one is trying to do or say at each stage in the discussion.

Match each intention with the corresponding part of the discussion.

SECTION 1   **SPEAKERS' INTENTIONS**

Introduces a second alternative.
Indicates a consequence.
Introduces a first reason.
Supports a reason.
Introduces a first alternative.
Introduces the topic for discussion.
Introduces a second reason.
Requests the opinion of the meeting.

INTENTION

General Manager   *Well, you've all read the preliminary report about the new organization. One of the most difficult problems is where to base the new group.*   a _____

One possibility is to move all headquarters' functions to Paris, and that is basically what the report recommends.   b   Introduces a first alternative.

Alternatively, we could continue to run the two companies quite separately in their present locations with only a small holding company in Paris.   c _____

I'm not sure how efficient the second option would be, but I'd like to hear your ideas on the subject.   d _____

Personnel Manager (Strasbourg)   *I'm afraid the people in Strasbourg aren't too happy about the idea of moving to Paris. For one thing, we've just completed work on a new headquarters building of our own at a cost of 25 million francs.*   e _____

But even more important in the eyes of the employees is the disruption of people's lives.   f _____

Nobody wants to move to Paris with its higher costs and big city problems.   g _____

If a move to Paris goes ahead, I won't be surprised if some people look for other jobs.   h   Indicates a consequence.

SECTION 2   **SPEAKERS' INTENTIONS**

Introduces one alternative.
Introduces a series of possibilities.
Gives an example to support an argument.
Requests an opinion.
Introduces a second alternative.
Presents his personal position.

INTENTION

General Manager	*Well, we've clearly got a problem here. What's your view on this, Jacques?*	a _____
Personnel Manager (Anker)	*I can see Martine's point of view, though obviously most of our people would have the opposite opinion since we are already Paris based.*	b Presents his personal position.
	But perhaps we could look at some other options. There seem to be at least two ways of dealing with the problem.	c _____
	One solution is obviously to move everything to Paris, as suggested, but, as we've heard, this will cause personal disruption and be expensive.	d _____
	But another possibility would be to separate some of the HQ functions and locate them in different places.	e _____
	For example, the Technical department and the Distribution department could easily be based in Strasbourg, with sales, marketing and administration in Paris. The personnel functions could also be divided between the two places.	f _____

SECTION 3   **SPEAKERS' INTENTIONS**

Gives a positive reason to support an argument.
Requests an opinion.
Contrasts a disadvantage against an advantage.
Shows agreement.

INTENTION

General Manager	*What do you think of that, Martine?*	a _____
Personnel Manager (Strasbourg)	*I'm much happier about that idea. I think there are a lot of advantages in maintaining the Technical and Distribution departments in Strasbourg, because most of the bottling plants are in the East of France.*	b _____
	And keeping some of the functions in Strasbourg means that our recent investment in a new building won't be wasted,	c _____
	whereas a total move to Paris would not make financial sense.	d _____

SECTION 4   **SPEAKERS' INTENTIONS**

Gives instructions.
Draws the discussion towards a close.
Presents one alternative and its consequence.
Indicates the next step in the decision.
Presents a second alternative and its consequence.

INTENTION

Financial   *Yes, I certainly agree with Martine. Either we keep the*   a _____
Manager   *Paris part of the HQ fairly small and therefore keep costs*
down,

or we move everything to Paris and cause a lot of   b _____
disruption and dissatisfaction. The choice seems pretty
clear to me.

General   *Good. There seems to be a consensus on this point.*   c Draws the
Manager   discussion
towards a
close.

What we should do now is work out how many people   d _____
would be involved in a move to Paris, and who would stay
in Strasbourg.

Check your
answers in the key.   *I'd like you two to give me a report on that by the end of*   e _____
the week.

Language   **Presenting different solutions**
Summary 1
During the meeting various alternatives were introduced
to solve the problem of where to base the headquarters of
the new group. This was done in several ways.

*One possibility is to move all headquarters' functions to
Paris.*

*Alternatively, we could continue to run the two companies
quite separately.*

*There seem to be at least two ways of dealing with the
problem.*

One solution is obviously to move everything to Paris.

*Another possibility would be to separate some of the HQ
functions.*

Either *we keep the Paris part of the HQ fairly small. . .,*
or *we move everything to Paris.*

Other phrases that can be used here are:

We could either. . .or. . .

One solution would be to. . ., or else we could. . .

As I see it, there are two possible solutions.

PRACTICE 1 Present a series of possible solutions to the following problems. Use the phrases above. Follow the example.

EXAMPLE

Problem:	How to link Denmark and Sweden by a bridge or tunnel.
Solutions:	• A rail tunnel with transport for cars.
	• A bridge only for road traffic.
	• A combined rail and road tunnel.

There are clearly several ways of solving this problem. One solution would be to build a rail tunnel with transport for cars. Alternatively, we could build a bridge just for road traffic. Finally, we could build a combined rail and road tunnel.

a Problem: How to make local industries more profitable.

   Solutions:
   • Introduce trade barriers.
   • Rationalize and streamline production methods.

b Problem: How to find new management personnel.

   Solutions:
   • Use a head-hunting agency.
   • Advertise in the national press.

c Problem: How to improve distribution of stock.

   Solutions:
   • Use one highly automated national warehouse.
   • Have a series of regional warehouses.

d Problem: How to improve productivity.

   Solutions:
   • Introduce more automation.
   • Organize employees into smaller teams.
   • Give bonuses for targets met.

e Problem: How to improve the quality of production

   Solutions:
   • Introduce quality circles.
   • Increase the sampling rate of finished products.

> Compare your versions with the ones in the key. They are on the cassette.

Language Summary 2

Justifying choices and alternatives

Also in the meeting several people gave reasons to justify one or other of the alternative solutions, sometimes arguing for and sometimes against. The following phrases were used.

For one thing we've just completed work on a new building. . .

But even more important. . .is. . .

If a move to Paris goes ahead I won't be surprised if some people look for other jobs.

(Moving everything to Paris) will cause personal disruption and be expensive.

Keeping some functions in Strasbourg means that our recent investment in a new building won't be wasted.

Other phrases that can be used here are:

The advantage of X is that. . .

Another advantage is that. . .

If we do X it'll have the advantage of. . .

By doing X we'll be able to. . .

PRACTICE 2

Read the following extract from another meeting at which the Personnel Manager of Anker France tries to convince the management of the Technical and Distribution departments that they should agree to move to Strasbourg. Complete the sentences with some of the phrases above.

Personnel Manager
So you see the best solution is to move to Strasbourg. (a) _____ most of the bottling plants are based in that part of France which (b) _____ you'll be near the points of production and distribution. (c) _____ that you'll be able to work more closely with the research group who are already based in Alsace.

Technical Manager
I can see the obvious advantages but there are clearly disadvantages. Moving to Strasbourg (d) _____ we'll be out of touch with our other colleagues in sales and marketing who will be based in Paris.

Distribution Manager
But apart from the professional side there's the personal aspect. Most of our families are settled in Paris and moving to Strasbourg (e) _____ a lot of disruption to children's education. (f) _____ is the fact that many of our wives or husbands have jobs in Paris, and they wouldn't be able to get new jobs if we moved. I can easily see some people leaving if the move goes ahead.

> Compare your version with the one in the key.

**Language
Summary 3**

Contrasting alternatives

One way to argue for one solution in favour of another is to contrast the benefits of one solution with the disadvantages of another. The following example is from the extract.

*Keeping some functions in Strasbourg means that our recent investment in a new building won't be wasted, **whereas** a total move to Paris would not make financial sense.*

Other ways to contrast alternatives are:

X means better profits. In contrast, Y could cause a lot of problems.

X would mean. . . On the other hand if we do Y it'll cause. . .

X would give certain benefits, but Y is much better from the company's point of view.

X does have some advantages. However there's no doubt that Y is a much better choice.

PRACTICE 3   Make contrasts between the following alternatives to problems, using the suggestions that are listed.

EXAMPLE

Problem: Where to locate the new offices.

Solutions: A: Move to a provincial centre – cheaper and more attractive for staff.
                B: Stay in London – expensive for rents and salaries.

Moving to a provincial centre would be cheaper and more attractive for staff, whereas staying in London is expensive both for rents and salaries.

a Problem: How to inform people of a new magazine.

  Solutions: A: Direct Mail – able to target with precision.
                  B: Advertising in the press – expensive and unsure of targets.

b Problem: Ways of getting photocopiers for a company.

  Solutions: A: Leasing – more flexible for upgrading, and better for cash flow.
                  B: Buying – ties up capital and difficult to change.

Compare your versions with the ones in the key. They are on the cassette.

6 Accepting and rejecting ideas and proposals

Aims   This unit shows the language used
- to accept ideas and proposals
- to reject ideas and proposals

Background

Bartletts, a British pharmaceutical and cosmetics company, produces an exclusive range of perfume and eau de cologne products and for many years their main product, *Charme,* has been one of the market leaders. However, increasing competition has changed this position, so they have recently launched a new perfume. A particular feature of the new product is the distinctive geometric shape of the bottles and the delicate kind of glass used. However, the new shape and material has created production problems as the existing printing machines are designed to print on the older, more conventionally shaped bottles.

 Comprehension Check

Listen to the extract of a meeting which took place to discuss the problem. Taking part in the meeting, in order of speaking, are:

Production Manager, Richard Dean.
Financial Manager, Martin Barham.
Marketing Manager, Diana Saunders.
Managing Director, David Fowler.

Decide if the following statements are **true** or **false.**

1   The Production Manager, who speaks first, wants to have a totally new machine.

2   The Financial Manager, who speaks second, agrees that a new machine is the best long term investment.

3   The Marketing Manager, who speaks third, wants to avoid new investment at this stage.

4   The Production Manager is unhappy about modifying the existing machine for use with the new product.

5   The final decision is to modify the existing machine.

Check your answers in the key.

 Focus on Language

Listen to the extract again and answer the following questions about the language used:

1   The Production Manager begins by proposing that they buy a new machine.
    a   Does he make his proposal in a weak or strong way?
    b   What phrases does he use? Complete the sentences:
    We _____ _____ _____
    _____ _____ _____ *invest in a*
    brand new printing machine.
    . . .you've _____ _____ *give me a printing*
    machine. . .

2   When the Production Manager puts forward his proposal
    for a new printing machine the Financial Manager rejects
    this.

    He uses two phrases which indicate that he is **strongly**
    opposed to the idea. What are they? Complete the
    sentences.

    . . .you know that that's _____ _____
    _____ *at present. . .*

    Any major investment in new machinery is really

    _____ _____ _____ _____

    at this stage.

3   When the Marketing Manager suggests modifying the
    existing printing machine the Financial Manager supports
    this idea. What does he say? Which word tells the listener
    that his support is strong? Complete the sentence:

    Yes, _____ _____ _____
    _____ *a better idea. . .*

4   The Production Manager still insists that a new machine
    is necessary. He politely rejects the idea of modifying the
    existing machine. What does he say? Complete the
    sentence:

    _____ _____ _____ _____

    _____ _____ _____ *that modifying*

    the old machine is a good idea.

5   The Production Manager insists strongly that the
    company should buy a new machine. What word in the
    following phrase indicates how strongly he feels.

    . . .a new machine's _____ _____

    _____

6   When the Production Manager tries to insist on the need
    for a new machine, the Managing Director again rejects
    the idea. However, he does this very diplomatically.
    What does he say? Complete the sentence:

    Well, _____ _____ _____
    _____ _____ *the problem but. . .*

7   The Production Manager reluctantly agrees to think about
    ways of modifying the machine. How do we know he is
    reluctant? What does he say?

    Well, _____ _____ *what can be done.*

> Check your
> answers in the key.

Focus on Intention
The full text of the meeting is given below divided into three sections. At the beginning of each section is a list of the different speakers' intentions – of what each one is trying to do or say at each stage in the discussion.

Match each intention with the corresponding part of the discussion.

SECTION 1   **SPEAKERS' INTENTIONS**

Puts forward a proposal.
Rejects a proposal.
Justifies a proposal.
Restates a rejection.
Justifies a rejection.

INTENTION

Production Manager	*Well, as I see it, we really have no option but to invest in a brand new printing machine.*	a _____
	If you want to print on these new bottles with their fragile surface and unusual shape, you've got to give me a printing machine specially designed for the job.	b Justifies a proposal.
Financial Manager	*Oh come on Richard, you know that that's just not feasible at present. Think of the cost.*	c _____
	Any major investment in new machinery is really out of the question at this stage.	d _____
	Our sales have been hit by increased competition and the general recession, and our whole profitability is in question.	e Justifies a rejection.

SECTION 2   **SPEAKERS' INTENTIONS**

Explains a suggestion in more detail.
Rejects a suggestion.
Restates a proposal.
Puts forward a suggestion.
Justifies a rejection.
Supports a suggestion.

INTENTION

Marketing Manager	*Why can't you try some kind of temporary modification to the existing machine?*	a _____
	In that way we'd be able to print on both types of bottle with no real additional costs.	b _____
Financial Manager	*Yes, that certainly would be a better idea from the financial point of view, and we . . .*	c Supports a suggestion.
Production Manager	*I'm sorry but I really don't think that modifying the old machine is a good idea.*	d _____

The new shape will cause all kinds of problems with feed-in and I reckon it'll mean a drop in productivity of at least 25%, with no guarantee of the results.

e _____

As I said before, a new machine's the only answer.

f Restates a proposal.

SECTION 3 **SPEAKERS' INTENTIONS**

Rejects a proposal.
Promises action.
Makes a request.
Makes a suggestion.

INTENTION

Managing Director

Well, I think we all appreciate the problem but I'm not happy about investing large sums of money on a separate printing machine.

a Rejects a proposal.

I really think we should all give this problem more thought.

b _____

Could you look into the practicalities of making some alterations to our existing print machine and come back to me with some ideas by next week?

c _____

Production Manager

Well, I'll see what can be done but I can't guarantee anything.

d _____

> Check your answers in the key.

Language Summary 1

Accepting proposals

In the discussion everyone accepted or rejected the various proposals, either strongly or diplomatically.

Note these ways of *accepting* a proposal or idea. The expression you choose will indicate to the listener the strength of your support. The strongest phrases come at the top. Those on the left are for use in a normal business situation. Those on the right are very informal.

Standard	**Informal**
I'm completely in favour of that.	*Great idea.*
I've absolutely no objections.	*Excellent.*
I'm sure that's the best solution/idea.	*Terrific.*
I'd be/I'm in favour of that.	*Good idea.*
That's a good idea.	*Sounds fine.*
That seems quite a good idea.	*Fine by me.*
I suppose that's OK.	*OK by me.*

PRACTICE 1   The following ideas have been put forward to improve overall office efficiency and motivation. Support the suggestions, using appropriate expressions, as indicated in brackets. Justify your support. The first one has been done as an example.

EXAMPLE

I think it'd be a good idea to change over from typewriters to word processors.
Reason: Makes that sort of work less repetitive. **(standard)**

Yes, I'm in favour of that. It would make that sort of work much less repetitive.

a   *What about advertising for someone to translate our technical literature?*
Reason: No one in the department has the time. **(informal)**

b   *I've been thinking it might be a good idea to introduce flexitime.*
Reason: Good for motivation. **(standard)**

c   *How would you feel about putting our mailing list onto computer?*
Reason: We should use the new micros more fully. **(standard)**

d   *Do you think we should increase our budget for training?*
Reason: People need to develop new skills. **(standard)**

e   *What do you think of giving everyone a basic computer awareness course.*
Reason: Computers are here to stay. **(standard)**

Compare your versions with the ones in the key. They are on the cassette.

Language Summary 2

Rejecting ideas

There were several examples in the meeting of people rejecting ideas and proposals, sometimes strongly, sometimes in a standard, polite way and other times very diplomatically.

. . . that's just not feasible. **(strong)**

I'm sorry, but I really don't think that. . . is a good idea. **(standard)**

. . . I think we all appreciate the problem but. . . **(diplomatic)**

Other phrases to use are:

Strong rejections

I really can't accept that.

I'm absolutely/completely against that.

That's out of the question.

Standard rejections usually begin with an apology

I'm afraid I can't accept that.

I'm sorry, but that's not really practical.

I'm afraid I'm not very happy about that.

I'm sorry, but I have reservations about that.

Diplomatic rejections

I don't want to be discouraging but...

I accept the need for a new machine but...

I appreciate your point of view but...

I can see why you want to do this but...

That's very interesting but...

PRACTICE 2   Reject the following proposals. Try to choose appropriate expressions as indicated in brackets and justify your objections.

EXAMPLE

Let's have a weekly departmental meeting.
Reason: take up time. **(standard)**

I'm sorry, but that's not really practical. It would take up too much time.

a   *What if we work an extra half hour every day so that we could leave early on Friday?*
.Reason: Need to be in office for visitors/calls.
(diplomatic)

b   *I suggest that we exhibit at the motor show in Geneva next year.*
Reason: Swiss market too small. **(standard)**

c   *Why don't we take on an extra marketing assistant for the new product launch?*
Reason: Need to train them. **(strong)**

d   *Why not try advertising for a marketing assistant in the local press?*
Reason: Coverage too small. **(strong)**

> Compare your versions with the ones in the key. They are on the cassette.

e   *What do you think of the idea of a "salesman of the year" competition to boost performance and motivation?*
Reason: Salesmen too cynical. **(diplomatic)**

Activity   Read the following description of a company problem and then discuss the list of proposals. Give reasons for your point of view.

A company which produces printed circuit boards is facing

a high rate of absenteeism among printed circuit board assembly workers and wants to reduce this over the next six months. Background information to the case is given below.

Key facts

- Average age of workers 30 (large % women).
- Work monotonous and staff turnover high.
- Order books full.
- Workers work 40 hour week (8.00–17.00), lunch break 30 min/two 15 min breaks.
- Area prosperous with many new factories.
- Workers take lunch in canteen shared with another company.
- Fairly strong union activity.

Proposals

- Get rid of top 5% of workers most frequently absent.
- Eliminate the breaks to save time.
- Increase automation to compensate for low productivity.
- Increase the amount of control of Doctor's certificates.
- Offer bonuses for the workers who are least absent.
- Give pay incentives or shares in company.
- Increase the working week to compensate for lost hours.
- Improve facilities e g nursery, new canteen.
- Appoint a special person to deal with social and home problems.
- Make factory more attractive, e g plant trees, provide rest rooms.
- Increase wages.

EXAMPLE DISCUSSION

A *What do you feel about the first proposal?*

B *I'm not in favour of getting rid of the top 5% of workers most frequently absent. There may be special reasons why, and what's more it would create problems with the union.*

No key.

7 Building up arguments

Aims This unit looks at language used to build up arguments for and against a case and in particular

- to give reasons
- to warn about negative results

Background   The context of the unit is the same as Unit 6. Bartletts, the British cosmetics company, has carried out the modification to the existing printing machine and the launch of the new perfume range has gone ahead. At first it sold well and then sales started to fall and after the first six months it seemed that the new product was going to fail. The marketing people blamed the inefficient production and consequent delays in delivery for the product's failure, and this raised the whole question of buying a separate machine again.

Comprehension Check   Listen to the extract of the meeting held to discuss the problem. Taking part in the meeting, in order of speaking, are:

Financial Manager, Martin Barham.
Marketing Manager, Diana Saunders.
Production Manager, Richard Dean.

Decide if the following statements are **true** or **false**.

1   The Financial Manager, who speaks first, wants to get a new machine as soon as possible to increase sales and cash flow.

2   Interest rates for borrowed money are high.

3   A lot of money has been spent promoting the new perfume range.

4   The Marketing Manager, who speaks second, feels that the new product will never have any chance of success unless a new printing machine is introduced.

5   The Production Manager, who speaks last, wants a new machine.

> Check your
> answers in the key.

 **Focus on Language**

Listen to the extract again, and answer the following questions about the language used.

1 The Financial Manager is against buying a new machine immediately. He gives two reasons:

   a What are they?

   b How does he introduce his reasons? Complete the sentences:

   _____ _____ _____ _____

   this year has been _____ *financially.*

   _____ *the new product has, to say the least, been*

   _____ *.*

2 He then puts forward his proposal to delay buying a new machine. How does he introduce his proposal? Complete the sentence:

   So _____ _____ _____

   _____ *that we put off any decision* _____

   _____ _____ _____

3 The Marketing Manager rejects the idea of putting off the decision.

   a What is her main reason?

   b How does she introduce this reason? Complete the sentence:

   That's impossible. _____ _____ *more delays.*

4 One consequence of failure to meet delivery dates will be that the new product will have no chance. How does the Marketing Manager introduce this consequence? Complete the sentence:

   We won't be able to meet our delivery dates _____ _____ *the new product will never have any chance of success.*

5 The Production Manager warns that any delay in buying a new machine will seriously affect production. How does he introduce his warning? Complete the sentence:

   _____ *we buy a new printing machine I just won't be able to guarantee production.*

6 Finally he makes a strong recommendation to replace it immediately. What are his words?

   We really _____ _____ _____

   _____ _____ *replace it immediately.*

> Check your answers in the key.

Focus on Intention

The full text of the extract is given below, divided into three sections as before. At the beginning of each section there is a list of the different speakers' intentions.

Match each intention with the corresponding part of the discussion, as in the examples.

SECTION 1   **SPEAKERS' INTENTIONS**

Illustrates explanation with evidence (2).
Offers a new proposal.
Rejects a proposal.
Adds a second explanation.
Justifies rejection with an explanation.

ARGUMENTATION

Financial Manager

Well, I can see why you want to buy a new printing machine, but I'm afraid it's just not possible right now.   a _____

Firstly, because so far this year has been disastrous financially.   b Justifies rejection with an explanation.

Sales are down and high interest rates have put an extra strain on our cash flow.   c _____

Secondly, the new product has, to say the least, been disappointing.   d _____

A fortune was spent on TV advertising, and sales have still been lower than expected.   e Illustrates explanation with evidence.

So, I can only suggest that we put off any decision until our position improves.   f _____

SECTION 2   **SPEAKERS' INTENTIONS**

Adds a conclusion.
Rejects a proposal.
Points out a consequence. (2)

INTENTION

Marketing Manager

That's impossible.   a _____

It'll mean more delays.   b _____

And as long as these delays continue we won't be able to meet our delivery dates,   c Points out a consequence.

and so the new product will never have any chance of success.   d _____

SECTION 3   **SPEAKERS' INTENTIONS**

Supports the previous speaker.
Makes a very strong recommendation.
Expands a point.
Warns of negative consequences.
Interrupts to add a point.

INTENTION

Production
Manager

Can I add something here?   a _____

Diana is quite right. Any further delay is quite out of the   b _____
question.

Unless we buy a new printing machine, I just won't be able   c _____
to guarantee production of the new products.

The modifications I carried out have put such a lot of strain   d Expands a point.
on the machine, I simply can't guarantee its reliability any
longer.

> Check your
> answers in the key.

We really have no alternative but to replace it immediately.   e _____

Language   **Giving a series of reasons**
Summary 1
In the meeting different ways of supporting or rejecting
proposals with a series of reasons were used.

I'm afraid it's just not possible. Firstly because. . .
Secondly. . .

Any further delay is quite out of the question. Unless
we. . .

The following phrases can also be used:

I'm against/for that proposal. . .

. . .because, first of all. . . and secondly. . .

First, due to. . . and secondly to. . .

One reason is. . . . Another is. . .

My first reason is. . . . My second is. . .

For one thing. . . . And for another. . .

PRACTICE 1 A major US car manufacturer intends to build a new plant somewhere in Europe and the following countries are the possible sites: Germany, Austria, France and Spain.

Accept or reject the proposals in favour of the different countries by using the information in the column on the right. Follow the example.

EXAMPLE

Proposal

In my opinion we should build the plant in Germany.

Information for your argument

Reasons against:

1 A well developed car industry

   Evidence
   Mercedes, Volkswagen, well established, sell well.

2 Wages very high

   Evidence
   Almost highest in Europe plus high social costs.

A *In my opinion we should build the plant in Germany.*

B *I'm sorry, but I don't think Germany's the right place. For one thing, Germany's already got a well developed car industry. Take Mercedes and Volkswagen, they're already well established and sell well. For another, wages are high, just about the highest in Europe and social costs are high as well.*

a *I believe the best site would be France.*

Reasons for:

1 Position good, near to other plants

   Evidence
   Existing plants in France and Belgium.

2 Highly skilled workforce

   Evidence
   Quality of French cars.

b *But what about the idea of building a plant in Spain, which is much cheaper?*

Reasons against:

1 Predict operating problems

   Evidence
   Lack of experienced car workers.

2 Isolated position

   Evidence
   Large distances between Spain and other existing plants, which are located in Northern Europe.

c *How about Austria as a site?*

Reasons for:

1 Not much competition

Evidence
No domestic car industry in Austria.

2 Potential market prospects

Evidence
Proximity to Eastern Europe –
potential market.

Compare your
versions with the
ones in the key.
They are on
the cassette.

3 Good history of industrial relations

Evidence
Few strikes compared to other
countries.

**Language
Summary 2**

Showing a series of consequences

The argument used by the Marketing Manager to argue
against further delay in buying the new printing machine is
summarized below in note form.

> Put off decision → More delays →
> Continuation of delays → Inability to meet delivery
> dates → No chance of success for the new product

Note how she connects the series of consequences into
a full argument:

*That's impossible. If we put off the decision, it'll mean more
delays, and as long as these delays continue, we won't be
able to meet our delivery dates, and so the new product will
never have any chance of success.*

Different ways of presenting a series of consequences are
given below.

If you put off the decision any longer,	*it'll mean* *it'll result in* *it'll lead to*	*more delays.*
As long as *If*	*these delays continue, we won't be able to meet our delivery dates.*	
And so *Therefore* *Consequently* *As a result*	*the new product will never have any chance of success.*	

PRACTICE 2   Reject the following proposals using the arguments presented below. Follow the example.

EXAMPLE

Proposal	**Argument against**	
Cut back on the training budget	less flexible workforce →	inability of company to modernize

A *I vote that we cut back on the training budget.*

B *I'm against that. If you cut back on training, it'll mean a less flexible workforce and if the workforce is inflexible it means the company won't be able to modernize.*

a Cut down on administrative paperwork	more errors with orders →	more complaints →	loss of customers
b Cut wages by 5%	lower standard of living for workers →	future high wage demands →	industrial action
c Increase taxation	people less motivated to work →	lower productivity →	lower company profits
d Lower retirement age	lack of experienced personnel →	more wrong decisions →	companies less successful

> Compare your versions with the ones in the key. They are on the cassette.

PRACTICE 3   Develop your own *chain* arguments to support the following ideas. Then compare your arguments with those of a colleague.

a The introduction of flexitime

b The introduction of quality control groups

c The introduction of more on-the-job training

PRACTICE 4   Develop your own *chain* arguments to reject the following. Then compare your arguments with those of a colleague.

a A shorter working week

b Wage controls and price freezes

c Nationalization of key industries

Language Summary 3

Warning about consequences

The Production Manager in the meeting emphasized his opposition to further delay in buying a new machine by giving a warning about the consequences. The following phrases can be used here:

Unless we buy / If you don't buy	a new printing machine,	I won't be able to guarantee production.
We must buy a new machine	or else / otherwise	

PRACTICE 5

Reject the following proposals using *If not/Unless/otherwise/or else*. You may have to change some words in order to keep the meaning the same. Follow the example.

EXAMPLE

Proposal
Raise our prices in line with inflation

Consequence
Lose our market share

I don't think that's very sensible. *If we don't keep our prices down, we'll lose our market share.*

or

I don't think we should do that. *Unless we keep our prices down, we'll lose our market share.*

or

That's not a good idea. We must keep our prices down *or else we'll lose our market share.*

a	Offer a 10% rise for the production workers	No money for investment
b	Reduce quality control to save money	More complaints and lose customers
c	Diversify production	Lose our reputation for specialist products.
d	Cut down number of management meetings	Breakdown in communication

Compare your versions with the ones in the key. They are on the cassette.

8 Summarizing and concluding

Aims   This unit looks at the language used

- to deal with interruptions and keep a meeting moving
- to summarize the main points
- to bring a meeting to a conclusion

Background

The context for this meeting is the same as Unit 1. INCA has recently introduced flexitime in the personnel and administration departments. This has caused resentment among the production staff, who do not work with flexitime, and a meeting has been held to discuss the problem. The first part of the meeting was heard in Unit 1, when we saw that the Production Manager and Personnel Manager had completely opposite opinions on the subject. The Managing Director must now try to find a compromise in order to resolve the matter, and prevent the threat of industrial action.

 Comprehension Check

Listen to the extract from the end of the meeting, in which two speakers are involved. These are, in order of speaking:

Managing Director, Graham Burns.
Personnel Manager, Anne Byron.

Decide if the following statements are **true** or **false.**

1   The Managing Director wants to introduce a new topic to the meeting.

2   He wants the Personnel and Production Managers to reach a compromise to the problem.

3   The Personnel Manager does not want to change the new flexitime arrangements in her department.

4   Productivity has increased because of the flexitime system.

5   Flexitime is good for staff morale and motivation.

6   The Managing Director wants some suggested solutions to the problem for later in the week.

> Check your answers in the key.

Focus on Language

Listen to the extract again and answer the following questions about the language used.

1   Before he brings the meeting to a close the Managing Director checks that everyone has presented their points. What does he say? Complete the sentence.

_____ _____ _____ _____

we ought to consider?

2   How does the Managing Director indicate that he wants to bring things to an end? What words does he use? Complete the sentence.

I'd like to _____ _____ _____

_____ _____ _____

and try to come to some decision.

3   He checks that both other members of the meeting agree that a compromise needs to be reached. How does he introduce this? Complete the sentence.

———————— ———————— ———————— *you both agree. . .*

4   The Personnel Manager is unhappy that she should have to reconsider the use of flexitime in her department. What does she say to show this? Complete the sentence.

———————— ———————— ———————— ————————

———————— ———————— ———————— *mistake. . .*

5   How does the Personnel Manager try to avoid answering the question about productivity increases in her department? What does she say? Complete the sentence.

Well, ———————— ———————— ————————

———————— ———————— *productivity gains. . .*

6   The Managing Director restates his decision that a compromise must be reached. How do we know that this is a restatement? What does he say?

7   At the end he checks twice that everyone agrees with his decision. What are the two phrases he uses?

8   What phrase does he use to bring the meeting to a halt?

> Check your
> answers in the key.

**Focus on
Intention**   The full text of this last part of the meeting is given below, divided into three sections. At the beginning of each section there is a list of the different speakers' intentions – what each speaker is trying to do or say at each stage in the discussion.

Match each intention with the corresponding part of the discussion.

SECTION 1   **SPEAKERS' INTENTIONS**

Directs the meeting to a finish.
Concludes and makes a proposal.
Summarizes.
Checks for agreement.
Checks that everything has been discussed.

INTENTION

Managing
Director   *Is there anything else we ought to consider now?*   a ————————

OK. If not, I'd like to go over what's been said so far and try to come to some decision.   b

Now, I've listened to both sides of the argument and we've discussed the difficulties of introducing flexitime in the production department.

c Summarizes.

I take it you both agree that this problem is serious and that some sort of compromise has to be worked out.

a Checks for agreement.

So I'm going to ask you to rethink the whole situation in the administration department, Anne, particularly with regard to the recent changes in starting and finishing times.

e _____

SECTION 2   **SPEAKERS' INTENTIONS**

Questions an opinion.
Defends a position.
Warns of consequence.
Disagrees.

INTENTION

Personnel Manager

I think that would be a big mistake, Graham. Just look at the advantages – motivation up, staff turnover down.

a _____

Managing Director

Yes, but can you really say you've got the increase in productivity you promised me?

b _____

Personnel Manager

Well, I'm sure you realize it's very difficult to measure productivity gains in administration.

c _____

But I can assure you, Graham, if you take away the flexibility my people have at the moment, the overall staff morale will drop dramatically.

d Warns of consequence.

SECTION 3   **SPEAKERS' INTENTIONS**

Restates conclusion.
Interrupts and redirects the meeting.
Proposes action.
Closes the meeting.

INTENTION

Managing Director

Well, I don't think we should discuss it further today.

a _____

As I said before there'll have to be some kind of compromise. I can't risk any disruption in production.

b _____

So, if there are no objections I suggest that you, Anne, go away and look at the problem and come back to me later this week with some suggestions.

c Proposes action.

Personnel Manager

If you say so, Graham.

Managing Director

Right if no one has anything else to add. . . .. Good, let's stop there, shall we?

d _____

**Language
Summary 1**

**Dealing with interruptions and irrelevancies, and
returning to the point**

Near the end of this meeting the Personnel Manager tries
to open up the whole argument about flexitime again. The
Managing Director manages to prevent the interruption, and
returns the meeting to the main point.

*Well, I don't think we should discuss it further today. As
I said before. . .*

Other useful phrases to use here are given below. They
range from formal (top) to informal (bottom).

*I take your point but can we please stick to the main
subject in hand.*

*I see what you mean but I think you're losing sight of the
main point.*

*That's all very well but I don't see what it's got to do with
the main point of this meeting.*

That's not the point. We're here to discuss. . .

OK, that's enough. Let's get back to the point.

These are other expressions which are useful to deal with
interruptions and indicate that the speaker is returning to
a previous point.

To go back to what I was just saying,. . .

To return to the main point,. . .

Going back to what I said before,. . .

Getting back to my original point,. . .

As I was saying,. . .

PRACTICE 1

In the following situations, there is an irrelevant
interruption. As the leader of the meeting, use the notes to
deal with the interruption and return to the point.

EXAMPLE

Situation:

A meeting is being held to decide if the
marketing department needs a 10%
increase in its advertising budget.

Interruption:

*I think we need to rethink our whole
approach to the media we use.*

Returning to the point:	That's all very well – not here to discuss advertising policy – go back to previous question – work out how to spend this extra money.
	That's all very well, but we're not here to discuss advertising policy. Going back to my previous question, can we look at how the extra money would be spent?
a Situation:	The company wants to reduce the number of personnel in the computer department.
Interruption:	*Did you read about the new laser printer being introduced in the States?*
Returning to the point:	Nothing to do with staffing levels – main point is to discuss staff reductions – return to previous point – what about outside software houses?
b Situation:	A multi-national company is planning to introduce a European advertising campaign. The different local country managers are meeting to discuss it.
Interruption:	*Did you see that advert for mineral water last week. – very quick off the mark?*
Returning to the point:	Not here to admire other adverts – return to main subject – three reasons for this new campaign – examine each one in detail.
c Situation:	A company is discussing the introduction of an electronic mail system for cheap and rapid communication between branches.
Interruption:	*I'm not too happy about the word processing software we are using at the moment.*
Returning to the point:	Deal with one point at a time – electronic mail is not directly related to word processing – choose the best electronic mail system first. – Perhaps look at the word processing question later.

> Compare your versions with the ones in the key. They are on the cassette.

Language Summary 2

Summarizing the main points

Before ending, the Managing Director summarized the main points, and the essential problem.

Now, I've listened to both sides of the argument and we've discussed the difficulties of introducing flexitime in the production department. I take it you both agree that this problem is serious and that some sort of compromise has to be worked out.

Other phrases that can be used to summarize points are:

So, to summarize, there seem to be three main problems. . .

So, we've discussed the problem of a new advertising campaign. Can we now try to reach a decision.

I think we've covered the three ways of improving our distribution system, and also the benefits of a new computer system. We've now got to decide on the best one.

PRACTICE 2

Summarize the points in the notes below as if you were ending a meeting. Follow the example.

EXAMPLE

Three main points – new pay levels, bonus scheme, profit sharing.

Well I think we've covered the three main points – new pay levels, the bonus scheme and a profit sharing scheme. Is that everything?

a 2 main problems – improving the quality level of our products; keeping the prices competitive.

b Advantages and disadvantages of the Sierra and Ascona as cars for sales reps – Sierra is cheaper to buy and insure but less reliable – Ascona is more expensive but comes out well on consumer tests.

c Main questions about business travel policy – is first class travel necessary – when is it necessary – should certain levels of staff never travel first class – should all personnel travel tourist?

d Three main points about new sales literature – full colour, light for mailing, response coupon for follow-up.

e Main questions about training premises
   – company training centre: expensive, convenient, purpose-built.
   – outside centre: cheaper, flexible, less convenient, less available.

Compare your versions with the ones in the key. They are on the cassette.

Language Summary 3

Coming to a conclusion

After summarizing the main points of the discussion, the Managing Director tried to come to a conclusion.

So, if there are no more objections I suggest that you...

Other phrases that can be used here are:

If everyone's in favour I suggest that. . .

If everyone's in agreement I propose that. . .

Then I recommend that. . .

Do you all agree that. . .?

Language Summary 4

Bringing a meeting to an end

After summarizing the main points, the Managing Director checked everything had been covered.

Is there anything else we ought to consider now?

Right, if no one has anything else to add. . .

Other phrases to check that everything has been said are:

Does anyone have anything else to add. . .? Right, then I think we can end the meeting at this point.

If nobody has anything to add then we can draw the meeting to a close.

So, if that's everything then we can stop here.

 PRACTICE 3

Use the notes below to come to a conclusion and then end the meeting. Follow the example.

EXAMPLE

Choose the Ascona for the sales reps.

Do you all agree that we should choose the Ascona for our sales reps? Does anyone have anything else to add? Right then, I think we can end the meeting at this point.

a The new car assembly plant should be in Spain.

b The profit sharing scheme should be implemented from next year.

c Our French agent should be changed immediately.

d The Middle East training contract is too risky at this stage in the company's development.

e Our distribution system should be reorganized using one central warehouse.

> Compare your versions with the ones in the key. They are on the cassette.

Key: Tapescript and answers

UNIT 1 TAPESCRIPT AND ANSWERS

Managing Director	Right, let's get started. As you know, we're just about to launch a major new product. But yesterday I was approached by a representative of our union, demanding an introduction of flexitime for their members and threatening some kind of go-slow. One department has already banned overtime and I'm afraid that we could have a strike on our hands before long. I've called this meeting firstly to look into ways of avoiding any further industrial action and secondly to review the whole situation regarding flexitime.
	Perhaps you'd like to start, Bob, and put us in the picture.
Production Manager	Well Graham, this morning I spent three hours with the unions and basically they want the same privileges as our administrative people. Frankly I don't blame them. They resent the fact that anybody with an office job can do exactly as they please.
Personnel Manager	Hold on, what do you mean by that? Are you implying. . .
Managing Director	Just a minute, Anne, let Bob finish what he was saying. We'll come to your point later.
Production Manager	Anyway, as I was saying, my people resent the fact that your department can walk in at ten in the morning when we've already done half a day's work. We have to be in the factory at seven, but your people can do exactly what they want.
Personnel Manager	What do you mean by that? You know very well that everybody works forty hours. The only difference is that they can come in any time between seven and ten.
Managing Director	Look, all this is very interesting but you're missing the point. The question is not whether flexitime is a valid concept but how we're going to avoid a strike.
	Now let's move on. Why can't we introduce flexitime in your production department?
Production Manager	Well, it's not that I've got anything against flexitime but you really can't introduce it at shop floor level. We have to keep

the assembly line moving at all times and it just wouldn't be possible to have people coming in when they please. The plant is old and any changes would mean extensive redesign.

Personnel Manager I'm sorry but that's hardly my problem. You can't expect me to drop a system just because you can't find ways of adapting. . .

Comprehension Check

1 True   2 False   3 True   4 True   5 False

Focus on Language

1 *Right, let's get started.*

2 *As you know,. . .*

3 *I've called this meeting* firstly to. . . and secondly to. . .

4 *Perhaps you'd like to start,* Bob, *and put us in the picture.*

5 *Hold on, what do you mean by that?*

6 *Just a minute Anne,* let Bob finish. . .

7 a *Look, all this is very* interesting but *you're missing the point.*

   b *The question is not whether* flexitime is a valid concept *but* how we're going to avoid a strike.

Focus on Intention

SECTION 1 b Presents a summary of the problem.
              d Directs the meeting to the first speaker.

SECTION 2 a Restates the problem.
              c Interrupts to control the meeting.
              d Returns to the original explanation of the problem.
              e Criticizes.
              f Counters criticism by explaining the situation.

SECTION 3 b Restates objectives.
              c Puts forward a suggestion.
              d Rejects a suggestion.
              e Explains rejection in greater detail.
              f Claims irrelevance.

PRACTICE 1 a Let's get going, shall we? Now you all know that we're being taken over by a big international firm who want to streamline the business. And we're here today to consider, first, some ideas for improving efficiency in the department and, secondly, the question of the introduction of new technology.

b Perhaps we'd better get started. As you know, interviews have to be held for the two vacant sales positions that we've got. So the purpose of our meeting today is to define exactly what we're looking for, and to draw up a shortlist of candidates.

c Well, I think we should begin. Now this trade delegation is arriving from Japan next month. So the main objective of this meeting is to draw up an agenda for the week of their visit, and to decide on a programme of social events.

d Right then, I think it's about time we got started. Some of you probably know that several complaints have been received recently about delivery delays. We're here today to find out first where exactly the delays happen, secondly what the causes are, and finally what the possible solutions are.

PRACTICE 2   a   g   b   c   e   f   d   h

As you know, John Saunders has applied for this senior post at HQ which became vacant last month. Three candidates plus Saunders have been interviewed, but he clearly has the greatest ability. He is very competent with excellent results after four years in the company. However, there is the problem of his lack of overseas experience. Basically the situation is this. 18 months ago we offered him a posting to North Africa, which he refused due to personal reasons – the ill health of his wife. He asked for a postponement of any overseas posting, and the Personnel Manager agreed to this. Then six months ago he was offered a post in France, and again he refused. His excuse again was the ill health of his wife. So the question today is. . .

PRACTICE 3   a   b   e   f   c   d

As you probably know, Anne Smith has indicated to me that she wants to leave the company. Now she joined the company two years ago, and in that time she's worked very hard and usually produced good results. However, recently I have noticed that she has been unable to meet deadlines, and is generally less enthusiastic and hardworking than before. Then two weeks ago she came to me and presented the following list of complaints – the pressures of her job are too great, the job is taking up too much personal time, leaving no time for friends and family. Some nights she works till 8 pm as well as on weekends. In addition she feels her salary isn't high enough. I'm reluctant to replace her as the company is small and very busy, and

I don't want to spend additional time training a replacement. She knows a lot about many aspects of the company, and it would take time for any new staff to obtain such a wide knowledge of the company. The question is, where do we go from here?

UNIT 2 TAPESCRIPT AND ANSWERS

Managing Director	What are your feelings on this government contract, John?
Marketing Manager	Well, personally I think we've got to avoid any contract which involves us with the Ministry of Defence. I mean we've got to consider public opinion.
Head of Research	I disagree completely. You're being too emotional about the whole thing. We've got to look at this objectively. As I see it, we're faced with a straight business decision. It's a choice between immediate but short term profits with the government and, on the other hand, developing a risky new product that may never earn the company any money.
Financial Director	And why not both? Take the case of Neco. They're involved in both types of business.
Managing Director	Yes, but you've got to remember that Neco is four times our size. I'm convinced we shouldn't rush into things that we may not be capable of doing. In my view trying to develop in too many directions would be madness.

It'll mean not only a huge injection of cash but also a large extension of our existing research facilities and we just don't have the money at the moment. |
Head of Research	In other words, you won't take the risk.
Managing Director	On the contrary, Philip, I'm only trying to do what is best for the company. We may be relatively small, but we do have a reputation for quality and I'm sure we'll lose it if we get involved in too many projects.
Head of Research	Maybe, but if there's more profit in going ahead with the government project, it seems to me that that's the direction we have to go in.
Financial Director	Exactly. You've got to think of our shareholders too. They're not going to accept years of low profits when they know you've had the chance of a contract that guarantees immediate profits for the next two years.
Managing Director	Well, I think we all need to think more about this whole matter, so I suggest we stop here and meet again tomorrow at eleven.

Comprehension Check   1 False   2 True   3 True   4 False   5 True

Focus on Language

1 *What are your feelings* on this government contract, John?

2 *Personally. . .*

3 *I disagree completely.* **(strong)**

4 *I'm convinced we shouldn't* rush into things. **(strong)**

5 It'll mean *not only* a huge injection of cash *but also* a large extension of our existing research facilities.

6 *On the contrary. . .*

7 *It seems to me that* that's the direction we have to go in. **(not very strong)**

8 Agrees. She says *Exactly.*

Focus on Intention

SECTION 1
b Gives an opinion.   e Gives an opinion.
c Expands his point of view.   f Expands his point of view.

SECTION 2
b Gives some evidence to support his case.
c Expresses reservation about an idea.
d Explains his point of view.
e Explains negative consequences.
f Criticizes.
g Disagrees.

SECTION 3
b Argues an opinion.   d Supports a point of view.
c Agrees.   e Closes the meeting.

PRACTICE 1
b *As I see it* **(neutral)**
c *I'm convinced* **(strong)**
d *In my view* **(neutral)**
e *I'm sure* **(strong)**
f *It seems to me that* **(tentative)**

PRACTICE 2
a From a financial point of view, expense account lunches can cost a company a lot of money.

b I think that giving gifts to customers as a method of securing orders is bad business practice, but in some countries it's the accepted custom.

c I'm inclined to think that companies which have adopted a policy of stopping all new recruitment as the main way to reduce costs and survive a crisis may be taking a shortsighted view of the problem.

    d It seems to me that the introduction of a system in which everyone in a company, from top to bottom, clocks in is very democratic.

    e I'm firmly convinced that more and more manufacturing industries will be transferred to the Far East because of lower labour costs.

    f The way I see it is that by the year 2000 world oil reserves will be running out and most of the energy will be supplied by nuclear power.

PRACTICE 3   **b** *Yes, but you've got to remember that Neco is four times our size.* (R)

    c *On the contrary, Philip, I'm only trying to do what is best for the company.* (D/S)

    d *Maybe, but if there's more profit. . .* (R)

    e *Exactly. You've got to think of. . .* (A/S)

PRACTICE 4   **a** Maybe, but having strong wage and price controls can also work well.

    b I wouldn't say that. The main point is that the type of work done by a secretary will change. She will be more like a personal assistant.

    c I quite agree. The future of manufacturing industries in Europe looks very bad.

    d That's not how I see it at all. The problem is much more complex than that.

    e I see your point, but I think things are slowly changing.

    f Precisely. Costs would go up and there would be no increase in productivity to compensate for it.

UNIT 3 TAPESCRIPT AND ANSWERS

Head of Research   I accept what you say about the problems with our image, but I still feel that this government project could be very interesting for us.

Managing Director   Yes, but on the other hand it would demand a lot of extra work on our part. There would be continual reports, meetings, checks and cross-checks which would waste e hours of everybody's time and create all kinds of extra administration. And what's more, we wouldn't have either the resources or money to pursue our own projects.

Marketing Manager   Yes, I agree totally with Nigel. Moreover, you've got to see that there's much more long term profit in developing the plant growth project. Of course, taking up the government offer may give a more immediate solution to our financial problem, but if there's a change in government policy and the project is cancelled or frozen, we'll be left with nothing at all. And another thing, we'll be getting into an area which is very dubious from an ethical point of view.

Financial Director I'm afraid you're being impractical, John. Although this work on plant growth rates may succeed eventually, it's too much of a gamble for us. If we concentrate all our energies in that direction we'll have to be prepared for unimpressive profits for at least the next few years, and even then there's no guarantee of success. Quite frankly, I don't think we'll survive that long without money coming in from other sources.

Managing Director Can I come in here, Helen? We seem to be losing sight of our objectives. If the company was in a real financial mess I'd have to agree with you – however, as I see it it's more a question of poor profits rather than a life and death struggle and the question is do we go for short term gains or look for a longer term strategy?

Comprehension Check

1 No. He has a better appreciation of the other point of view, although he still favours the government project.
2 It would mean too much extra administration, and it would take money and resources away from other projects.
3 The company's own project for developing ways of speeding up plant growth.
4 Government policy could change and the project could be cancelled. It is also dubious from an ethical point of view.
5 The company's own project on plant growth rates.

Focus on Language

1 *I accept what you say about* the problems with our image, but...
2 Yes, *but on the other hand* it would demand a lot of extra work...
3 And *what's more*, we wouldn't have either the resources...
4 *Moreover*
5 ...but *if there's a change in government policy* and the project is cancelled or frozen, *we'll be left* with nothing at all.
6 *Although* this work on plant growth rates *may* succeed eventually, it's too much of a gamble...

Focus on Intention

SECTION 1   **a**   Shows understanding of another point of view.
  b   Puts forward an opposite point of view.
  c   Points out a disadvantage.
  e   Gives an additional reason.

SECTION 2   **a**   Shows agreement.
  b   Adds an extra reason.
  c   Points out a possible consequence.

SECTION 3   **a**   Disagrees.
  b   Balances an advantage against a disadvantage.
  d   Presents a firm opinion.

PRACTICE 1   **a**   The relocation of offices to smaller centres certainly creates a better working environment but it can make recruitment more difficult.

  b   Although the fall in interest rates makes borrowing cheaper and is good for industry, it also affects the exchange rates which makes essential imports like oil more expensive.

  c   Rationalizing traditional heavy industries like steel or coal improves productivity, but on the other hand, it also creates an unemployment problem.

  d   Import controls help national industries and domestic manufacturers. However, they can encourage domestic manufacturers to become more uncompetitive.

PRACTICE 2   **a**   I don't agree with the idea of using more robots in industry. Although they probably lead to an increase in productivity, they also lead to unacceptable levels of unemployment.

  b   I don't think that direct taxation should be increased. Of course it creates more revenue for the government in the short term, but on the other hand it decreases the motivation of companies and individuals.

  c   I'm against the idea of relaxing exchange controls. I can see that it may encourage international trade and investment. However, it would allow money to leave the country for investment abroad.

  d   I'm not convinced that flexitime should be more common in companies. Although it gives employees more independence, it also creates administrative and staffing problems.

PRACTICE 3   1   **a**   if   **b**   it will cause/create
              c   may   **d**   will lead to
              e   if   **f**   could/may

PRACTICE 4

a If they stop production immediately and recall all supplies, it will seriously affect their cash flow.

b If they decide to ask for more investigation into the chemical while they maintain production, it may lead to lawsuits from customers in the future.

c Holding a meeting with employees to tell them of the situation will certainly stop the rumours in the company, and will be good labour relations.

d If we write an article in the house journal denying everything, it could be very dangerous, especially if the chemical is harmful.

PRACTICE 5

a Word processors are definitely more efficient than typewriters. Not only can you change text easily but you can also store information.

b There should be less emphasis on nuclear power. There's a big danger of accidents and apart from that you have the problem of all the waste material.

c Companies should think more about reducing their energy consumption. First, there's the high price of oil and electricity, and in addition there's the long term danger of using up oil stocks.

d I'm against open plan offices. First of all they're very noisy, and what's more, there are a lot of distractions.

UNIT 4 TAPESCRIPT AND ANSWERS

European Commercial Manager   As you know, we have to take some hard decisions about the size and shape of the new company, and I'd like to hear some of your suggestions. First of all, about the reorganization of the marketing department. Can you give us the background, Hervé?

Marketing Manager (Anker)   Yes, well you all know that Anker (France) is divided into three divisions for marketing purposes – retail, that's shops and supermarkets; bars and cafés; and restaurants and large hotels. Societé de Boissons Gazeuses on the other hand, has only two divisions – retail; and bars, cafés, restaurants and hotels. Our suggestion is that the new group marketing structure should reflect the existing Anker one.

European Commercial Manager   What's your reaction to that, René?

Marketing Manager (Strasbourg)	I'm afraid I don't agree with Hervé. The main point of this meeting is to look at ways of rationalizing the company, and in my opinion the two division structure that we have is much more efficient than Anker's three. But there's no real difference between the bar and café sector, and restaurants and hotels – the form of distribution is the same, so is the packaging. We think that the three division structure has too many overlaps. So we strongly recommend that the new company should be modelled on our two division structure.
European Commercial Manager	That sounds like a very valid point about overlap of functions. Don't you think that your three division structure might be more expensive to operate, Hervé, especially in a bigger company?
Marketing Manager (Anker)	I don't think so, Andrew. It's just a question of splitting resources into three parts, and it enables us to give each market sector more personal service.
Marketing Manager (Strasbourg)	Before we take any decision it would be a good idea to compare the cost of sales between the two companies for the different sectors. I'm sure that would prove that the two division structure is the only solution. . .

Comprehension Check

1 True   2 False   3 True   4 True   5 True
6 False

Focus on Language

1 *I'd like to hear some of* your suggestions.

2 *Can you give us the background,* Hervé?

3 *Our suggestion is that* the new group marketing structure *should* reflect the existing Anker one.

4 *What's your reaction to that,* René?

5   a   Politely
    b   *I'm afraid I don't agree with* Hervé.

6 So *we strongly recommend that* the new company *should be modelled* on our two division structure.

7   a   René's opinion
    b   *Don't you think that* your three division. . .?

8 it *would be a good idea* to compare the cost of sales.

9 I'm *sure that* would prove that the two division structure *is the only solution.*

Focus on Intention

SECTION 1

  b   Requests suggestions.
  c   Introduces the topic for discussion.
  d   Invites someone to speak.
  f   Makes a recommendation.

SECTION 2
   a Requests an opinion.
   b Disagrees.
   d Supports his argument.
   f Makes a recommendation.

SECTION 3
   a Expresses tentative agreement.
   c Disagrees.
   d Gives reasons to support his opinion.
   f Gives a strong opinion.

PRACTICE 1
   a Well, our objective this year is to improve productivity without extra investment in equipment. How do you think we should do this?

   b The problem we've got is how to keep pay rises within government limits, and at the same time to maintain the motivation of the workforce. Do any of you have any suggestions?

   c We need to find a way of expanding the business without losing control or borrowing large amounts of money. I think we should consider franchising. What do you think?

   d Don't you think that the idea of getting all managers over 50 to retire early would leave the company without valuable experience?

   e As fuel costs have risen, this obviously affects distribution costs. Do you think we should increase our prices?

   f Well, I think we all agree that the company needs to change its image from that of a traditional safe insurance giant to a dynamic financial services group. How do you think we should do this?

PRACTICE 2
   a I think we should investigate road transport as an alternative. It might also be a good idea to set up small regional warehouses.

   b First of all, we must withdraw all tins from the shelves. Then we should arrange a meeting with the production people from the Spanish plant. And we could send some of our production people to Spain to check quality control.

   c I strongly recommend that we increase our bid. In addition, I recommend that we should try to buy more shares privately. And have you thought of writing to the other company's shareholders?

   d The first thing we must do is to send a consultant to investigate progress. And it might be a good idea to establish a deadline for results. Or what about taking a participation in the company?

e I would suggest that we hire a new editor, as the first step. Then I think we have no alternative but to negotiate with the print unions to modernize production methods.

UNIT 5 TAPESCRIPT AND ANSWERS

General Manager
Well, you've all read the preliminary report about the new organization. One of the most difficult problems is where to base the new group. One possibility is to move all headquarters' functions to Paris, and that is basically what the report recommends. Alternatively, we could continue to run the two companies quite separately in their present locations with only a small holding company in Paris. I'm not sure how efficient the second option would be, but I'd like to hear your ideas on the subject.

Personnel Manager (Strasbourg)
I'm afraid the people in Strasbourg aren't too happy about the idea of moving to Paris. For one thing, we've just completed work on a new headquarters building of our own at a cost of 25 million francs. But even more important in the eyes of the employees is the disruption of people's lives. Nobody wants to move to Paris with its higher costs and big city problems. If a move to Paris goes ahead, I won't be surprised if some people look for other jobs.

General Manager
Well, we've clearly got a problem here. What's your view on this, Jacques?

Personnel Manager (Anker)
I can see Martine's point of view, though obviously most of our people would have the opposite opinion since we are already Paris based. But perhaps we could look at some other options. There seem to be at least two ways of dealing with the problem. One solution is obviously to move everything to Paris, as suggested, but, as we've heard, this will cause personal disruption and be expensive. But another possibility would be to separate some of the HQ functions and locate them in different places. For example, the Technical department and the Distribution department could easily be based in Strasbourg, with sales, marketing and administration in Paris. The personnel functions could also be divided between the two places.

General Manager
What do you think of that, Martine?

Personnel Manager (Strasbourg)
I'm much happier about that idea. I think there are a lot of advantages in maintaining the Technical and Distribution departments in Strasbourg, because most of the bottling plants are in the East of France. And keeping some of the functions in Strasbourg means that our recent investment

in a new building won't be wasted, whereas a total move to Paris would not make financial sense.

Financial Manager Yes, I certainly agree with Martine. Either we keep the Paris part of the HQ fairly small and therefore keep costs down, or we move everything to Paris and cause a lot of disruption and dissatisfaction. The choice seems pretty clear to me.

General Manager Good. There seems to be a consensus on this point. What we should do now is work out how many people would be involved in a move to Paris, and who would stay in Strasbourg. I'd like you two to give me a report on that by the end of the week.

Comprehension Check

1 True   2 False   3 False   4 True   5 False
6 True

Focus on Language

1 *One possibility is* to move. . .

2 *Alternatively, we could* continue to run. . .

3 *For one thing,* we've just completed. . .

   But even more important in the eyes of the employees *is the disruption* of people's lives.

4 There *seem to be at least two ways of dealing* with the problem.

5 *One solution is obviously* to move everything to Paris.

6 *But another possibility would be* to separate. . .

7 Keeping some functions in Strasbourg *means that* our recent investment in a new building *won't be wasted, whereas* a total move to Paris *would not make financial sense.*

8 *Either* we keep the Paris part of the HQ fairly small and *therefore keep costs down, or* we move everything to Paris and *cause a lot of disruption and* dissatisfaction.

Focus on Intention

SECTION 1

a Introduces the topic for discussion.
c Introduces a second alternative.
d Requests the opinion of the meeting.
e Introduces a first reason.
f Introduces a second reason.
g Supports a reason.

SECTION 2

a Requests an opinion.
c Introduces a series of possibilities.
d Introduces one alternative.

e Introduces a second alternative.

f Gives an example to support an argument.

SECTION 3
   a Requests an opinion.
   b Shows agreement.
   c Gives a positive reason to support an argument.
   d Contrasts a disadvantage against an advantage.

SECTION 4
   a Presents one alternative and its consequence.
   b Presents a second alternative and its consequence.
   d Indicates the next step in the decision.
   e Gives instructions.

PRACTICE 1
   a As I see it, there are two possible solutions. We could either introduce trade barriers, or on the other hand we could rationalize and streamline our production methods.

   b There are at least two ways of dealing with this problem. One possibility is to use a head-hunting agency. Alternatively, we could advertise in the national press.

   c There seem to be two ways of solving this problem. We could either use *one* highly automated warehouse, or we could have a series of regional warehouses.

   d There seem to be at least three ways of solving this problem. One solution is obviously to introduce more automation. Another possibility is to organize employees into smaller teams. Or thirdly, we could give bonuses for targets met.

   e As I see it, there are two ways of dealing with this problem. One possibility would be to introduce quality circles. Alternatively, we could increase the sampling rate of finished products.

PRACTICE 2
   a For one thing   **b** means that
   c Another advantage is   **d** means that
   e will cause   **f** Even more important

PRACTICE 3
   a Direct mail means that we'll be able to target with precision *whereas* advertising in the press is expensive and we would be unsure of reaching our targets.

   b Leasing is more flexible for upgrading, and better for cash flow whereas buying ties up capital and it's difficult to change the machine.

UNIT 6 TAPESCRIPT AND ANSWERS

Production Manager	Well, as I see it, we really have no option but to invest in a brand new printing machine. If you want to print on these new bottles with their fragile surface and unusual shape, you've got to give me a printing machine specially designed for the job.
Financial Manager	Oh, come on Richard, you know that that's just not feasible at present. Think of the cost. Any major investment in new machinery is really out of the question at this stage. Our sales have been hit by increased competition and the general recession, and our whole profitability is in question.
Marketing Manager	Why can't you try some kind of temporary modification to the existing machine? In that way we'd be able to print on both types of bottle with no real additional costs.
Financial Manager	Yes, that certainly would be a better idea from the financial point of view, and we. . .
Production Manager	I'm sorry but I really don't think that modifying the old machine is a good idea. The new shape will cause all kinds of problems with feed-in and I reckon it'll mean a drop in productivity of at least 25%, with no guarantee of the results. As I said before, a new machine's the only answer.
Managing Director	Well, I think we all appreciate the problem but I'm not happy about investing large sums of money on a separate printing machine. I really think we should all give this problem more thought. Could you look into the practicalities of making some alterations to our existing print machine and come back to me with some ideas by next week?
Production Manager	Well, I'll see what can be done but I can't guarantee anything.

Comprehension Check

1 True   2 False   3 True   4 True   5 False

Focus on Language

1   a   in a strong way.
    b   We *really have no option but to* invest in a brand new printing machine.
      you've *got to* give me a printing machine. . .

2   you know that that's *just not feasible* at present. . .
    Any major investment in new machinery is really *out of the question* at this stage.

3   Yes, *that certainly would be* a better idea. . .

4   *I'm sorry but I really don't think* that modifying. . .

5   a new machine's *the only answer.*

6 Well, *I think we all appreciate* the problem but. . .

7 Well, *I'll see* what can be done.

Focus on Intention

SECTION 1 **a** Puts forward a proposal.   **c** Rejects a proposal.
d Restates a rejection.

SECTION 2 **a** Puts forward a suggestion.
b Explains a suggestion in more detail.
d Rejects a suggestion.
e Justifies a rejection.

SECTION 3 **b** Makes a suggestion.   **c** Makes a request.
d Promises action.

PRACTICE 1 **a** Good idea, because no one in the department really has the time.

b I'm completely in favour of that. It'll be very good for motivation.

c I've absolutely no objections, and we should start to use our new micros more fully.

d I'm sure that's the best solution, especially as many people need to develop new skills.

e That seems quite a good idea, and computers are certainly here to stay.

PRACTICE 2 **a** I can see why you want to do this but we still need to be in the office to receive visitors and take calls.

b I'm sorry but I have reservations about that. The Swiss market is really too small to justify it.

c That's out of the question. We'd need to train them and that would just take too long.

d I'm completely against that. The coverage we'd get would be too small compared to national advertising.

e I don't want to be discouraging but I think that the salesmen are too cynical to respond to that idea.

UNIT 7   TAPESCRIPT AND ANSWERS

Financial Manager Well, I can see why you want to buy a new printing machine, but I'm afraid it's just not possible right now. Firstly, because so far this year has been disastrous financially. Sales are down and high interest rates have put an extra strain on our cash flow. Secondly, the new product has, to say the least, been disappointing. A fortune was spent on TV advertising, and sales have still been lower than expected. So I can only suggest that we put off any decision until our position improves.

Marketing Manager That's impossible. It'll mean more delays. And as long as these delays continue we won't be able to meet our delivery dates, and so the new product will never have any chance of success.

Production Manager Can I add something here? Diana is quite right. Any further delay is quite out of the question. Unless we buy a new printing machine, I just won't be able to guarantee production of the new products. The modifications I carried out have put such a lot of strain on the machine, I simply can't guarantee its reliability any longer. We really have no alternative but to replace it immediately.

Comprehension Check

1 False   2 True   3 True   4 True   5 True

Focus on Language

1 a The company has had a bad year financially.
    The new product has not sold very well.
  b *Firstly, because so far* this year has been *disastrous* financially.
    Secondly, the new product has, to say the least, been *disappointing.*

2 So, *I can only suggest* that we put off any decision *until our position improves.*

3 a It will cause delays in meeting delivery dates.
  b *It'll mean* more delays.

4 . . .dates *and so* the new product will never have any chance of success.

5 *Unless* we buy a new printing machine, I just won't be able to guarantee production.

6 We really *have no alternative but to* replace it immediately.

Focus on Intention

SECTION 1 a Rejects a proposal.
      c Illustrates explanation with evidence.
      d Adds a second explanation.
      f Offers a new proposal.

SECTION 2 a Rejects a proposal.
      b Points out a consequence.
      d Adds a conclusion.

SECTION 3   **a** Interrupts to add a point.

              b Supports the previous speaker.

              c Warns of negative consequences.

              e Makes a very strong recommendation.

PRACTICE 1   **a** I believe the best site would be France.

Yes, I agree with that. One reason is its good position, near to other company plants elsewhere in France and in Belgium. Another is the existence of a highly skilled workforce, which is shown by the quality of French cars.

b But what about the idea of building a plant in Spain, which is much cheaper?

I'm afraid I'm not in favour of that idea. First of all, because there are likely to be severe operating problems due to the lack of experienced car workers. Secondly, because of distances between Spain and the company's other existing plants which are located in Northern Europe.

c How about Austria as a site?

Yes, that's an interesting possibility. For one thing, there isn't much local competition as there's no domestic car industry. Secondly, there are potential market prospects in Eastern Europe. Finally, there's Austria's excellent record of industrial relations, with fewer strikes compared to other countries.

PRACTICE 2   **1** **a** I think we must cut down on administrative paperwork.

I'm afraid I don't agree with you there. If we reduce the paperwork too much, it'll lead to more errors with orders, which in turn will result in more complaints and probably a loss of customers.

b One way to get out of this present financial problem is to cut wages by 5%.

That's out of the question. It would mean a lower standard of living for our workers and will definitely lead to high wage demands in the future, with the probability of industrial action.

c The best way to increase government revenue is to raise taxation.

I'm not sure you're right about that. Increasing taxes will result in people being less motivated to work, and if there is less motivation then productivity will go down, and so you will have lower company profits and less corporation tax.

d One solution to unemployment is to lower the retirement age.

I don't agree with that idea. It'll mean a lack of experienced personnel in important positions, which could lead to more wrong decisions being taken, and as a result companies will be less successful.

PRACTICE 5 a That's out of the question. Unless we keep our wage costs down, we won't have money for investment in new equipment.

b I don't agree with that at all. We've got to maintain our high level of quality control, otherwise we'll get complaints from customers and may lose some of them.

c I'm not in favour of that idea. If we don't keep to our present production range, we'll lose our reputation for specialist products.

d That's not a good idea in my view. We've got to have regular management meetings or else there'll be a breakdown in communication.

UNIT 8 TAPESCRIPT AND ANSWERS

Managing Director Is there anything else we ought to consider now? OK. If not, I'd like to go over what's been said so far and try to come to some decision.

Now I've listened to both sides of the argument and we've discussed the difficulties of introducing flexitime in the production department.

I take it you both agree that this problem is serious and that some sort of compromise has to be worked out.

So I'm going to ask you to rethink the whole situation in the administration department, Anne, particularly with regard to the recent changes in starting and finishing times.

Personnel Manager I think that would be a big mistake Graham. Just look at the advantages – motivation up, staff turnover down.

Managing Director Yes, but can you really say that you've got the increase in productivity you promised me?

Personnel Manager Well, I'm sure you realize it's very difficult to measure productivity gains in administration. But I can assure you, Graham, that if you take away the flexibility my people have at the moment, the overall staff morale will drop dramatically.

Managing Director Well I don't think we should discuss it further today. As I said before, there'll have to be some kind of compromise. I can't risk any disruption in production.

So if there are no objections, I suggest that you, Anne,
go away and look at the problem and come back to me later
this week with some suggestions.

Personnel   If you say so, Graham.
Manager

Managing   Right, if no one has anything else to add. . . (Not at the
Director   moment). . . Good, let's stop there, shall we?

omprehension   **1** False   **2** True   **3** True   **4** False   **5** True
Check   **6** True

Focus on
Language

1 *Is there anything else* we ought to consider?

2 I'd like to *go over what's been said so far* and try to come to some decision.

3 *I take it* you both agree. . .

4 *I think that would be a big* mistake. . .

5 Well, *I'm sure you realize it's very difficult to measure* productivity gains. . .

6 *As I said before,* there'll have to be some kind of compromise.

7 *So, if there are no more objections. . .*
Right, if no one has anything else to add. . .

8 *Good, let's stop there, shall we?*

Focus on
Intention

SECTION 1   **a** Checks that everything has been discussed.
   b Directs the meeting to a finish.
   e Concludes and makes a proposal.

SECTION 2   **a** Disagrees.
   b Questions an opinion.
   c Defends a position.

SECTION 3   **a** Interrupts and redirects the meeting.
   b Restates conclusion.
   d Closes the meeting.

PRACTICE 1   **a** That has nothing to do with staffing levels. The main point of this meeting is to discuss staff reductions. Returning to my previous point, what about using outside software houses?

   b That's all very well but we're not here to admire other adverts. If we return to the main subject, I can see three reasons for this new campaign and I'd like to examine each one in detail.

    c I see what you mean but can we deal with one point at a time. Electronic mail is not directly related to word processing. I think we should choose the best electronic mail system first, and perhaps we can look at the word processing question later.

PRACTICE 2   **a** So, to summarize, there are two main problems – improving the quality level of our products, and keeping the prices competitive.

    b Well, I think we've covered the main advantages and disadvantages of the Sierra and Ascona as cars for sales reps. Basically, the Sierra is cheaper to buy and insure but less reliable; the Ascona is more expensive but comes out well on consumer tests. We've now got to take a decision.

    c The main questions to ask about our business travel policy are the following. Is first class travel necessary, and, if so, when is it necessary? Should certain levels of staff never travel first class, or should all personnel travel tourist? Let's start with the first point.

    d So, we've all agreed on the three main points about our new sales literature. It should be full colour, light for mailing and with a response coupon for follow-up. Are there any other points we should consider?

    e The main questions to ask about training premises for the company are: Should we build our own centre, which would be expensive but would also be convenient and purpose-built? Or should we use an outside centre, which would be cheaper, more flexible, but also perhaps less convenient and not always available?

PRACTICE 3   **a** Are you all agreed that the new car assembly plant should be in Spain? If nobody has anything to add then we can draw the meeting to a close.

    b If everyone's in favour I suggest that the new profit sharing scheme should be implemented from next year. So, if that's everything then we can stop here.

    c If everyone's in agreement I propose that our French agent should be changed immediately. Does anyone have anything else to add? Right, then let's stop here.

    d Do you all agree that the new Middle East training contract is too risky at this stage in the company's development? Right, if no one's got anything else to add I think we can end the meeting here.

    e Are we all agreed that our distribution system should be reorganized using one central warehouse? So, if that's everything then we can stop here.